# EXTRAORDINARY

SPECIAL EDITION

---

*The Remarkable Life Of*

*Bishop Hardy Lee Coleman Sr.*

---

# By Suellen Estes

IHHI

Hutchins House Publishing Co. LLC
Blue Mountain, MS

Hutchins House Publishing Company, LLC
Blue Mountain, Mississippi 38610
http://hutchinsmarketing.us

I dedicate this book to

The generations of the
Coleman, Starks, and Harris Families
who have followed Bishop Coleman
into a life of service to Jesus.
May you never forget your noble heritage,
and may you all continue to carry this magnificent
torch you have been handed.

# A special thanks to:

**Bishop Hardy Lee Coleman, Sr. and**
**First Lady Ann Harris Coleman**
I have been incredibly blessed by the time we have shared during the writing of this book.

**Bishop Coleman's children: Lottie Clarke, Mary Ruth Nesbit, Carnelia Barnes, Hardy Coleman, Jr., Dwight Coleman, and Mildred Chills**

**Mother Ann Coleman's children: Louise Williams, Elaine Wherry, Linda Williams, and Jerry Harris**

**All of the Leaders in the Global Pacific Diocese of the Church of the Living God**

**Mississippi State Elder Henry Jeans, Illinois State Elder Hardy L. Coleman, Jr., District Elder Jeremiah Simmons, District Elder Wylie Starks, Elder Garnie Freeman, Elder Adrian Ivy, Elder Maurice Loving, Elder Terry Macon, Elder Leo Robins, Elder Troy Starks, Elder Carey Williams, Elder Gail Williams, and Mississippi State Secretary Annette Gray**

All of you have been so generous in spending time with me as I attempted to get a glimpse into the extraordinary life of Bishop Coleman. The stories and comments you have shared have made this book possible. I will be forever grateful.

A special thanks to my husband,

**Mickey Estes**

Your prayers and spiritual insights have encouraged me, and your creativity and technical skills continue to amaze me.

# Contents

# Introduction

The air seemed to be filled with electricity as we stepped across the mosaic tile crosses on the floor of the foyer, and entered the huge sanctuary. We walked down the carpeted aisle of the splendid room and chose some seats close to the front - not wanting to miss anything. As we slipped into the padded chairs and settled ourselves in, we glanced around. There was elegance everywhere.

Of course, there was the elegance of the building itself, with every detail carefully planned. From the lighting, to the expansive stage with its beautifully designed pulpit chairs, to the podium from which would be released powerful messages, to every detail - excellence prevailed.

What was most impressive, however, was the elegance of the people. Fine suits, fashionable dresses, elaborate hats, jewelry, and radiant faces were everywhere. Anticipation was in the air.

This event was for all ages – from the elderly to tiny children. Little girls with immaculately braided hair and little boys with their pint-sized ties seemed right at home as they chased each other between the rows of chairs. Mothers and fathers snapped their fingers, bringing correction and order. Then as the boys tucked their shirts back in, and the girls straightened their hair bows, these younger ones nestled into their seats to await their favorite part: the energetic praise which was soon to come.

This was indeed a family affair. Generations, as a matter of fact. There were grandparents, aunts, uncles, cousins - all dedicated to a life of living for the Lord. These were those who truly knew their God, and it showed. It was clear that all ages honored this event as significant. They had come to worship God, and to grow in their understanding of His Word. His blessing upon these families was evident.

The convention of the Global Pacific Diocese of the Church of the Living God was about to begin. The band struck its first chords, the choir stood up, and exuberant praise filled the room. My eyes welled with tears as I joined in the singing. Magnificent music. Magnificent praise being lifted up to God. What an experience!

Many churches had come together for this occasion, but there was one leader of them all, Bishop Hardy Lee Coleman, Sr. My mind wandered, realizing that every single person in this room – and many more rooms, for that matter, had been directly influenced by this one man. Quite a few of these people were his relatives – generations who were raised up to know and honor

Jesus. There were many other families, of course, but they all had this one thing in common. Bishop Coleman had touched their lives significantly.

How does one man come to have so much impact on others? What does he possess that equips him for such great influence? What does he do that causes that influence? What can others learn from this great man which will help them to have more productive lives for the Lord? These are questions which I would like to answer in this book.

Extraordinary is the story of a remarkable man of God: a man who has been in ministry for 73 years. (Now 92 years of age, Bishop Coleman has been in the ministry since he was 19). Of course, on one level, to share his story of rising from a sharecropper in a segregated south to becoming the leader of many, is inspirational in itself. Yet my prayer is that as you read, you don't see this as just one great man's story, but as a life which could be an example for you. His love of God, his faithfulness to his call, his faithfulness to his family, his compassion for others, his whatever-it-takes attitude, and his holy life are qualities which we could all emulate.

So as you join me on this journey through the life of a great man, I hope that you are blessed and inspired as much as I have been.

Come with me and meet an Extraordinary Man.

*I will praise thee; for I am fearfully and wonderfully made: marvellous are thy works; and that my soul knoweth right well.*

*Psalms 139:14*

# 1

## Early Years

"Run! Run! Don't Stop! Run!"

Gasping and panting, the two young men charged ahead, moving away from the enormous wall which seemed to be chasing them. What was it? Where did it come from? No time for questions now, they just had to get to safety.

A tsunami-like wall, about 100 feet tall, was racing toward them - a wall of dust being carried by the howling wind. Everything in its path was engulfed by the whirling dust. They had never seen anything like this.

The torrent swirled around them as they ran, carrying with it the dirt which was quickly overtaking everything. "Head for the ditch!" was the next directive. As the two fell on their knees, unable to see, they clutched the wire fence, hanging on with all their might. The wind and dirt still swirled, but at least they could somewhat cover their faces, as they waited for this strange force to abate.

Hardy Lee Coleman and his friend had just encountered one of the strangest of phenomena. They had encountered the great dust storm of 1937. From the bone-dry dustbowl of Oklahoma to the drought-ridden farms of the south, whirling winds had churned and carried the dust in such a way that the effect was almost tornado-like. Very strange, indeed.

About a half hour later, the wind had subsided and visibility had returned. The entire landscape seemed to be covered with a thick powder. Clothes, shoes, hair – everything - had been covered by the yellowish dust.

Still trembling from the terrifying experience, the tall, lanky, Hardy rose to his feet to survey the scene – and the damage. All of the corn which they had been thinning was part of the yellow powdered landscape – yellow, and suffering from the beating which had occurred. Reddish yellow because of all of the clay soil which had been stirred up and placed in other locations, and beaten down because of the powerful wind. No need to continue this job today; they needed to go home. Perhaps Hardy's mother would need him.

---

*But every challenge which came Hardy's way seemed to be one which allowed his exceptional character to shine through.*

---

This episode was one of many dramatic moments which would be in young Hardy Coleman's life. He had already experienced disappointments which might have severely damaged the psyches of weaker boys. But every challenge which came Hardy's way seemed to be one which allowed his exceptional character to shine through.

He was an overcomer. He was a natural-born leader. In the days ahead, many would see what kind of person he was. They would see that he was extraordinary.

### It Was A Different Time

To understand this man's story, you have to understand the culture into which he was born and raised. Hardy was a black boy raised in the segregated rural south, long before Martin Luther King, Jr. came on the scene.

There was a structure in place, and everyone lived by it. Few even questioned it. That's just the way things were, and the separation of people, which had grown out of the slave culture …well, I'll say it again, that's just the way things were.

White and black people went to different schools, different restaurants, and even different churches. They had separate public bathrooms, separate water fountains, and separate seating in the theaters. All of this seems unfathomable today, but in the early 20$^{th}$ century, it was just "normal."

When money was hard to come by for the white man, it was doubly so for the black man. Most of the black people depended on farm labor or domestic jobs in order to survive. When things were tight, and these jobs were scarce, life really got tough.

## A Child Was Born

So on May 20, 1922, when Hardy Lee Coleman was born in a small log cabin on the John Peeler farm, on a dirt road, in Benton County, Mississippi, few people realized the significance of the moment. He was just another black baby born to a poor family on a farm. But God knew the significance, of course. He had special plans for this man. He was one-of-a-kind, and over the next several years this fact would unfold very clearly. He had an incredible future in store. But not just yet.

**Fred (Bud) Coleman**

Hardy's parents, Fred (Bud) and Willer Timsy Davis Coleman, were "sharecroppers," so they lived on the farm where they worked. (For those who aren't familiar with the term, sharecroppers were those who would work the farms for the richer landowners or renters. Their pay would be a portion of the harvest). There had been an older sister, Lottie, but she had died before Hardy was born. His family was smaller than most: just he and his parents.

As was the custom with many families in those days, as soon as Hardy could engage in any work at all, his skills would be included in the operation. So some of his first memories are picking, pulling, or loading the crops with his father. It was hard work for a boy. It required lots of endurance over the long hours of manual labor.

This was before the days of modern farm equipment. No motorized equipment was available. So the work was done by hand. Handheld hoes and plows pulled by mules. These were the instruments of the day. Hard, hard work, indeed.

19

During those early years, the family moved in with his father's family where they would be more comfortable.

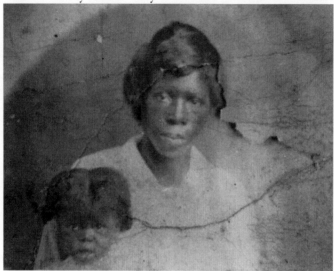

**Willer Timsy Davis Coleman and Lottie**

Grandfather Coleman was a likeable chap, a deacon in the church nearby... and a first class moonshine still operator. Young Hardy would occasionally take a peek at the still which was hidden in the garden – a place where law enforcement officials would never think to look. So his business was safe during those days of prohibition. Nobody seemed to notice the discrepancy between Grandpa's "church days" and the rest of the week.

## Days In The Life Of A Farm Boy

The greatest point of safety and security for the young children of Benton County was their home. The immediate family was the center of their lives, and the extended family added that boost of confidence and inspiration. There were lots of music, fun, and laughter as the families came together after the hard day's work.

As young Hardy grew, he enjoyed life. "It wasn't so bad," he'll say. "We always had fun with the other children around." The grownups would talk and laugh and enjoy each others' company.

The families would walk along the dusty roads, chatting with neighbors as they went. They walked to work. They walked to school. And they walked to church, or to visit with neighbors. Few automobiles were available.

**Troubled Times**

It seemed to be a day like any other. Hardy and his dad had worked alongside some others in the field, until they were bone tired. Mopping their faces with their handkerchiefs, the two trekked toward home. Happy to have accomplished so much, Hardy felt very satisfied, but thirsty. Stopping to drink some water from his neighbor's well, the young boy chatted amicably with his friend before making the final distance to his house.

When he entered the house, the atmosphere was different. His mother was crying and wringing her hands, and there was stress on his dad's face. Something strange was happening, but Hardy wasn't sure what it was.

21

He had heard some sharp words lately, but he thought that was normal. His father seemed to be complaining a lot, but they were all working hard, so that was to be expected.

What was happening on this day had not been expected. In fact, it was unthinkable. His father was announcing that he was leaving the family. He wanted freedom from the responsibility of his family, so Hardy and his mother would be on their own. Young Hardy was shocked!

Moving out of his grandfather's house was really hard for young Hardy. There had been a sense of security with the older people around. Now things were totally different. From now on, young Hardy would be the man of the house... and he was only twelve years old. Too young for such responsibility, but he would have to rise to the occasion.

Sad times.

As young Hardy and his mother found a sharecropper's house in which to live, they began to establish their new routine. At only 12 years old, Hardy was the chief bread winner, so he had to work more diligently than ever in the fields. Not much time to play – or to go to school, because his work was what brought provision for himself and his mother. Mrs. Coleman took a job as a housekeeper, but Hardy was the one who brought in most of the income. His life had changed suddenly, but he was willing to accept the challenge.

This sudden change was one of many "suddenlies" which would come to Hardy's life.

One day, while rocking on his front porch, enjoying the cool breeze after a day's work, Hardy had a strange experience. There was no one else around, and he was enjoying a few moments alone. Suddenly his name rang out as clearly as if a person were speaking it. "Hardy," he heard. But there was no one there; it seemed to be coming from the air. "Hardy." So he answered, "Yes." He knew that the Holy Spirit had spoken his name, and he had answered.

---

*This sudden change was one of many "suddenlies" which would come to Hardy's life.*

---

Fear set in. He had heard that if the Spirit called your name and you answered, you would die. So the young man sat there waiting. Waiting to die, or at least waiting to see if what had been told him was true. Hardy sat there amazed, having answered the Holy Spirit, and not having died. He felt very special.

This was the first of many unusual encounters young Hardy would have with the Holy Spirit. God had special plans for this young man, and those plans would become clearer as he went along.

But not just yet.

*Early Years*

*Before I formed thee in the belly I knew thee; and before thou camest forth out of the womb I sanctified thee, and I ordained thee a prophet unto the nations.*

*Jeremiah 1:5*

# 2

## Teenage Transitions

As teenage years developed, life continued as "usual" for the time. Hardy and the teenage girls would be eyeing each other in the fields, at school, or as they walked along the country roads. Sometimes the guys would share some cigarettes – or some beer or moonshine. They would tell stories and pull pranks. The girls would vie for the attention of the young guys and vice versa. Sometimes they would slip around and let their chosen person know – maybe even slipping a kiss. During those days, there were many young girls with their eyes on the handsome Hardy. Hardy, in return, would enjoy the attention – and engage in flirting with them also.

But as we've said before, God had special plans for this young man. Even though at the time Hardy didn't realize his call, there seemed to be a supernatural protection which would keep him out of the trouble some of his friends encountered.

When Hardy turned 18, everything changed. The last six years he had spent as chief bread-winner for himself and his mom, so he was much more mature than many of his peers. All of his responsibility had caused him to grow in character and discipline. He had to be faithful to his work and to the administration of the finances which came in.

Little did he know that during this time he was being groomed for something greater. He was being groomed for a responsibility in God's kingdom...and the time was approaching when he would be ready.

**A Call From His Maker**

How is it that a young boy from rural Mississippi hears the call of his Creator to step up to a higher plane in life? What makes him decide to give up the status quo and live a life for God?

---

*Little did he know that during this time he was being groomed for something greater.*

---

These questions are hard to answer. Hardy had not been brought up in a Christian home. His mother was kind to him and had tried to instill character into him, but she was not a devout Christian. Maybe the hurt of his father leaving caused his heart to be tender. Maybe it was all of the responsibility of providing for himself and his mother at such an early age. For whatever reason, Hardy Coleman was different from his peers, and that was about to be demonstrated.

There had been hints of God's pull, as Hardy had noticed some of the people who were walking with Jesus. Quite an awakening had broken out in the country surrounding him, and people had taken notice of some strange occurrences.

Sometimes when people felt the Holy Spirit upon them, they would cry out, "I'm sanctified!" or they would shout, "Hallelujah!" Hardy always took notice when that happened. He could tell that they were experiencing something quite different, and he was curious about it. Maybe someday he would like to have that experience, but not now.

One morning, as he was getting dressed, something *really* caused him to take notice. His aunt, who was not much older than he, had quite a reputation - and not a good one. She liked to party, and most of his friends were well aware of that.

Suddenly, with no prior warning, he heard his aunt shout in the next room, "I'm sanctified!" Hardy couldn't believe his ears! He knew "how she was," and she definitely wasn't considered a saint, so when she had this encounter, he couldn't get it out of his mind. Indeed, strange things were happening. Why would his aunt be encountering the Holy Spirit? She wasn't a "church lady."

The next morning, with his aunt's experience still on his mind, Hardy stretched out across his bed and started praying. He knew that he would someday want to have such an experience with God, but not now. He had too much to do. Hardy decided that he would wait until he was about 40 years old. That would give him enough time to fulfill all of his own dreams, and then he would follow God.

Yet the young man's heart was truly softening toward his Creator.

There was a church meeting going on at Booth's Chapel that night, and he decided to go. At first, he got distracted by some friends who wanted to slip off down the road and smoke cigarettes. But he wasn't distracted for long. As the crowd of young boys slipped away, he started with them, and then pulled back. There was a distinct nudge from his Creator to attend the meeting.

As Hardy entered the meeting, he surveyed the scene. Quite a commotion was occurring in the school building where the church met. People were singing, clapping, and shouting. They did that for awhile, seeming to enjoy the moment, even though it seemed to Hardy like it went on too long.

Finally the preacher stood up and delivered his message, calling for the people to come and give their lives to the Lord. To Hardy's surprise, his mother, who wasn't a Christian, went down to the front to receive prayer for healing. Hardy was totally intrigued by what was happening, but he wasn't convinced that this was for him. Not yet, anyway.

Then came "the song" which seemed different from all the others. There was a power in the air as all of the people began to sing, "Let Those Refuse To Sing Who Never Knew Thy God." As Hardy stood there, rigid and silent, God's voice prodded him, "Why aren't you singing?" So, reluctantly, Hardy started to sing, and as he sang out with the others, this teenager had a change of heart. A power greater than himself seemed to take over, and as if he were dreaming, he found himself walking down the aisle to the front of the church.

The young man began to pray. "Lord, I believe I'll try."

That's all God was waiting for: His permission to invade this special young man's life. Everything of Hardy's past went before his eyes, and he began repenting – promising to give up this thing and then that. Tears filled his eyes as he saw the wrongs which he had committed. He truly wanted Jesus to wash away the past and let him begin anew.

The things which happened next seemed really strange to Hardy. He seemed to fall asleep for a few seconds, and when he awoke, he found himself shouting and speaking in an unknown language. Hardy had never heard of anyone speaking in tongues, but he was doing it, and somehow, he knew that this was God. What in the world was happening to him? God was making Himself known in a most powerful way, and Hardy Coleman was being forever changed as he was filled with the Holy Spirit.

---

*That's all God was waiting for: His permission to invade this special young man's life.*

---

Bishop Coleman still remembers this event, as if it happened yesterday. "It was like flipping a switch," he says. "It's as if I went to sleep, and woke up another person." He is still not sure what had caused him to go to the front for the meeting that night. It had to be the powerful draw of God's Spirit.

On May 28, 1940, at age 18, Hardy Lee Coleman had become a believer – a "new creature," according to scripture. *Old things had passed away and all things had become new.* (I Corinthians 5:17) No longer would he be smoking with the boys, or trying to kiss the girls, but he would be following after Jesus for the rest of his life. There would be obstacles ahead, and trying times, but nothing would be able to take away this relationship with Jesus, which had just begun.

Nothing at all.

Friends don't always understand such transformation, and neither did Hardy's. But they respected him, and began to hold him in high esteem. Now when they were sneaking cigarettes and beer, they didn't expect him to participate. He was better than that.

The night he walked down the aisle was Hardy's first act of obedience to the Lord, but there would be many others. Years and years of obedience would follow. Years of stretching and growing into God's vision for him. At 18 years of age, Hardy Coleman had just begun a lifelong journey which would take him to places that he could never imagine.

As part of the change, prayer became very important. Hardy wanted to know this great God who had called him to this new life, so he would often go out into the woods, alone, and spend time praying and listening. It was quiet there, and he wouldn't be disturbed.

About a year went by before Hardy's next significant encounter. He was out in the woods where it was beautiful and peaceful. The tall trees were rustling softly in the breeze and birds were chirping their messages to each other. Hardy was praying. He wanted all that God had for him, and he wanted to do all that God desired of him.

The Holy Spirit began to speak in what seemed like a booming voice. The words were so powerful, they seemed to shake the very ground on which he was standing. "Go into all the world and preach the gospel, and declare that the time won't be long," resounded in his heart. Hardy stood in the silence which followed.

**The Clump of Trees Where Hardy Was Called**

A new mantle had been offered to him, a new assignment. What should he do? He knew in his heart that there was only one thing he could do. He answered, "Yes, Lord," and young Hardy's path was set before him. As he answered that call, Hardy had no idea where that path would take him, but he knew that it was the voice of God calling him to preach, and his answer was simple. "Yes, Lord, I'll do what you say."

As Hardy left the woods that day, he seemed to be trembling with the awesomeness of the moment. His mother, Willer, had received the Holy Spirit on the same night as Hardy, so she was excited at her son's call. Both of them had spent the last few months in continual amazement at the reality of God's presence in their lives. Now this call from God generated incredible excitement for them both.

Hardy had already shared with his friends every chance he could get. Now he was going to begin sharing messages to the groups in the churches which were springing up. The news went out that Hardy was called to preach, and pastors began inviting him to speak.

Today when you hear the word, "church," you often envision a building, but not in those days. There weren't any pentecostal church buildings in Hardy's community. "Churches" met in homes or in school buildings. So it was in an old house, at a gathering of believers, where Hardy delivered his first sermon. "Many Signs and Wonders" was the title, as he brought the Book of Acts into rural Mississippi. He gave a charge to the people, "*You* write a sign. *You* take the message. *You* be a sign and a wonder to those around you."

A car, covered with a white sheet drove back and forth in front of the house. The occupants shot guns into the air, trying to scare the worshipers. These lawless ones wanted to put a stop to the message which was emboldening its recipients. But they didn't stop Hardy. What God had started couldn't be stopped by man or Satan.

## The Path

*Trust in the Lord with all your heart, and do not lean on your own understanding. In all your ways acknowledge Him, and He will direct your paths. (Proverbs 3:5-6)*

The book of Proverbs gives us understanding about two paths which one could choose. There is the path *which seems right unto man, but the end of it is death. (Proverbs 14:12)* Then there is *the path of the righteous, which is like the light of dawn. It shines brighter and brighter til the noon day sun. (Proverbs 4:18).*

Starting out, the first path is the easy one. You just go with the flow and do what everyone else is doing. On that path, you put yourself and your desires on the throne of your heart, and proceed to fulfill those desires. It may "seem right," but sooner or later there will be huge regrets.

The second path requires wisdom. It isn't as easy at first. Faith, discipline, and obedience to God's Word are necessary. But as you move along this path, it will become clearer as you go, that you have chosen well. That's where God's blessings are. That's the path which builds happy families and fruitful lives for the kingdom.

Hardy Coleman, still in his teen years, chose the second path - the road less taken. While many of his friends were just hanging out, he was praying and studying God's Word. He was preaching wherever he could.

He was also looking for God's choice for his wife.

*Whoso findeth a wife
findeth a good thing, and
obtaineth favour of the Lord.*

*Proverbs 18:22*

# 3

## The Preacher Gets A Bride

Ezera Starks was recognized as the prettiest girl in the neighborhood, and lots of the boys had their eyes on her. They would come to her house, trying to get her attention... but her father, Cane Starks, kept an eye out for her well-being and her safety. He was a believer, and a holy man. He wanted only the best for his daughter.

Hardy had noticed her, along with the other boys, before he got saved, but she wasn't interested – and neither was her father. Ezera wasn't just pretty, she had high standards to go along with her beauty.

On the night Hardy received the baptism in the Holy Spirit, Ezera was in the meeting, and completely skeptical when she saw the young man going forward to get saved. "What does he think he is doing?" she said to her friend next to her. It seemed that he was mocking the event. She had seen him around, and he seemed to be quite a prankster. He couldn't be serious about the Lord.

But he *was* serious, and was she ever shocked to see the results of Hardy's encounter! He truly did mean it, and he truly was a changed man. Incredible!

Ezera liked the new direction in Hardy's life, and she began to notice his transition. She saw him reject the flirtations of some of the more worldly girls, and she saw him earnestly seeking to learn more about God. She was especially impressed when he began preaching.

Hardy made his interest known, and the two began courting. Then about two years after his conversion, on June 27, 1942, the young couple got married. Both families were happy over the match. By this time, Hardy's mother had grown in her walk with the Lord – and even her own healing ministry. Ezera's family members were also counted with the believers. So this new holy couple made a terrific pair.

Ezera's family had suffered severely from the prejudice of the era. Her father, Cane Starks, had been raised by a white woman – something which was quite unusual at the time. The reason was also unusual. Cane's mother had given birth to a baby which had been fathered by a white man. There was so much outrage against such that she had been forced to leave the county, in fear of her life.

Interracial marriage was absolutely taboo – in fact, it was against the law. Though there was no retribution for the white man, the black woman paid a huge price, and was forced to desert her son. So the compassionate Rosa Smith took Cane to raise, since his mother wouldn't be able to care for him.

So Ezera was accustomed to hearing about racial drama, but what happened to them on their wedding day was totally unexpected. The young couple exchanged their wedding vows on a June afternoon, and that night attended a revival service at Booth Chapel.

During the service, some white men invaded the meeting, relishing guns, and severely beat the preacher, Pastor Rapier. Needless to say, things became chaotic as the attendees began to scurry. The white men then grabbed young Hardy, putting a gun to his head, and demanded that these meetings be stopped. Shaken by the event, the young newlyweds left the service and went home, but more determined than ever to follow the Lord's will. Men couldn't stop what God had started.

Later the truth came out about this raid: race wasn't behind this onslaught, but religion was. The men had been sent by some black deacons from another church.

Jealous over the successful meetings which were being conducted, with many getting saved and filled with the Holy Spirit, they wanted the evangelism to stop. God's move of the Spirit had threatened their own power structure.

Another type of prejudice had risen to attack these on-fire believers.

Mockingly, these new believers, so full of God's Spirit, were called "saints." They were shunned by many – even Christians - and persecuted by others. God was on the move, and the devil didn't like it! Ezera's father was one who paid the price of his commitment - being evicted by his landlord because he was a "saint." Some of those who didn't understand this new phenomenon, would attack the converts wherever they could.

---

## It was like the Book of Acts being revisited.

---

In the meantime, God's awakening continued, many lives were changed, and many were healed. Excitement was in the land about God's Holy Spirit.

In this new community of believers, the people would stand together. If they were forced away from one place, they would just go to another and continue their worship. Some of those who had been first to believe would mentor the ones who came later. And if any family needed special prayer, there were many who would gather around to join in. It was like the Book of Acts being revisited.

## A Change Comes Suddenly

Hardy's life seemed to be marked by what you might call "suddenlies." He suddenly had responsibility thrown upon him when his father left home. He suddenly had a new life with the Lord when he was radically saved at 18. He suddenly had his call to preach thrown his way at 19. Now in his twenties, he was to encounter another huge "suddenly." He was to become a pastor.

From the time of his conversion, Hardy and Ezera had been mentored by a special pastor and his wife. In fact, to this day, Hardy holds up Sister Susan Rapier as one of the greatest saints he has ever known. Her faith was unstoppable, and her love for others brought dozens to the Lord.

Pastor Gene and Sister Susan Rapier oversaw three churches: Booth's Chapel (where Hardy received his salvation), Perry's Chapel, and Bald Knob. Since the churches were scattered between two counties, the Rapiers had to travel back and forth every week,

**Mother Rapier**

preaching and caring for their members.

Some events transpired which caused Pastor Rapier to resign from his post, and suddenly, with no prior warning, Hardy Coleman was called to be the pastor of these three churches. If he accepted the position, he would be a husband, father of a growing family, sharecropper, sawmill attendant, preacher - and pastor of three churches. A lot of responsibility for a man who was only 26 years old.

Once more, Hardy rose to the occasion. He felt that he knew nothing about pastoring a group of people, but trusting the Lord had become a habit with him and Ezera. Once again, he accepted the challenge which came his way, and a new phase of ministry began. In 1948, Hardy Coleman was established as Pastor.

The Colemans' lives were busy – and often very tiring. Yet all of the time, this young pastor and his wife were growing in their understanding of God – and of His people. Pastor Hardy was learning how to lead them with love and compassion, but also with encouragement to be true disciples. Not only would he have the messages to bring each week to the three congregations, but often his congregants would need prayer and encouragement as they were meeting life's challenges during the week. Times were indeed busy.

The hardest part of the pastor's mission was to deal with the arguments which would arise. Self-centered people, whether they are church members or church leaders, are prone to strife and divisions. And it was no different in these early years with these rural churches.

When people truly allow the Spirit of God and His Word to invade their lives and develop their character, strife is not the norm. However, when people are seeking their own way, strife is commonplace.

Some of the pastors were jealous of Pastor Hardy's success. And some of the church members often had jealousy or anger toward each other.

**Booth Chapel L-R; Deacons Jack Crawford and Charlie McKenzie with Pastor Hardy Coleman**

Yet through all of this, Pastor Hardy pressed forward

and continued to lead the three congregations. This was God's call, and he would be faithful to it.

## The Coleman Family Develops

The next twenty years were incredibly busy and demanding for the Coleman family. During the first thirteen years of their married life, Ezera gave birth to eight children. They still lived in sharecropper houses, as Hardy – and Ezera (when she could), worked the farms. During this time, they moved around from farm to farm – always seeking a better wage, and better living conditions. Yet all of the houses were rustic, with no running water or electricity. Four rooms to house the whole family, which became increasingly hard as the family grew.

During the winter months, when farming wasn't providing a living, Hardy would add to their livelihood by cutting wood for a sawmill – using hand equipment – no power saws. Hard work.

Yet every Sunday he would be preaching somewhere – always working for the Lord. Many times, as he preached, there would be little or no offering, but he wasn't doing it for the money. There was one church which had not given him much of an offering for several weeks. On a certain Sunday they raised a huge offering for the time: $700. Excited for his family to receive some of the things they needed, the young preacher was surprised to learn that the administrators had given $200 of it to the parking attendants. Not much was left, but it was still more than usual for the family.

The Colemans were learning to walk by faith. They believed in God's supernatural power and provision – the power to heal – and the provision they needed for their welfare. They worked hard, and as was the custom, the children would join in the labor on the farms they were tending. (Sometimes even having to miss school to accomplish their tasks). Together this family was learning to worship God, to be thankful for all things, and to be diligent in their daily lives. Sometimes they may have felt poor, but really they were very rich. They were storing up treasures which could never be taken away from them.

---

## *The Colemans were learning to walk by faith.*

---

Day by day, month by month, and year by year they were growing in wisdom and in favor with God. They were seeking together the highest life available – the life with Jesus truly being their Lord.

*Lo, children are an heritage of the Lord: and the fruit of the womb is his reward.*

*Psalms 127:3*

# 4

# Life In Benton County

If you were to drive down a certain dirt road in Benton County, Mississippi in the summer of 1951, you would encounter some interesting sights. Sure, the car in front of you would inhibit part of your view because of the dust it stirred up, and your rear view mirror would signify that you were making your own cloudy contribution. That's just the way it was, driving on the roads of Benton County.

Yet between the dusty episodes, you would see life – and lots of it, out in the cotton fields you would pass. Old and young, male and female, people would be out picking the cotton, and bringing in the provision for their families. Some would be mopping their brows from the heat of the sun. Others would be fanning away the sweat bees which loved to swarm around the workers.

At the side of the field, you might see Lottie, now 7 years old, and old enough to help with the babysitting chores. Some of the church people who wanted to work had small children, so Pastor Hardy would say, "Bring them and put them on the pallet. Lottie will watch them for you." So Lottie, along with Carnelia and Mary Ruth, would play with the babies and try to keep them pacified.

Lottie was the Colemans' oldest daughter, and very responsible. Besides, she loved looking after the children and playing with them. What she hated was the field work. She hated the bees and the hot sun. And she hated the back-breaking work of bending and picking.

Last year when she was working hard out in the field, her brother Bobby had scolded her for not picking her share. Bobby was only a year and three months older, but he was tall and muscular, and seemed to pick three hundred pounds just like that. Not Lottie. It was harder for her, so she would make an excuse of going to the house

**Ezera with Bobby, Lottie, and Carnelia**

and bringing water for everyone. Bobby just didn't understand!

At the first of this summer, Hardy, Jr. had been born: the sixth child of the Coleman family. Bobby was now 8, Lottie 7, Carnelia 5, and Mary Ruth 3. The girls had discovered that there was a baby on the way when they were getting something out of the dresser drawer. Mama had made some new baby clothes! "We're going to have another baby!" It was always fun to have another baby to play with. Bobby wasn't quite as excited, but he would love his little brother when he came.

The saddest time ever had come to the Coleman household the year before. After three daughters, Pastor Hardy had been really excited to have another son when Jimmy Dee was born in 1949. He was a joy to the whole family. As he grew, he seemed to have a special affinity for his dad. One of his first words was "Da Da," and he would make the church people laugh when he would call to his dad as he preached.

When Jimmy Dee was about 14 months old, he contracted a virus – which developed into pneumonia. As he got sicker and sicker, Pastor Hardy, Ezera, and Pastor's mother – along with all of the church people prayed for him. This time healing didn't come, and young Jimmy Dee died.

The other children were so young that they couldn't bear the burden of all of this, so Ezera didn't even tell them as soon as it happened. They found out when a neighbor came out to their car as it passed and told them how sorry he was. The girls quickly turned to see if their mother was carrying the baby, and when they saw that she wasn't, they knew that it must have been true.

Pastor Hardy was devastated over the death. The older children gathered at the window and watched as he sat on a board hanging between the trees outside. Their father was crying uncontrollably, as Ezera rubbed his back. She was being strong for him this time. The loss of a child was so hard to take.

So when Hardy, Jr. was born this year, everyone was thrilled that he was a boy. He was strong and healthy – and fun for the whole family.

Next year Lottie would be old enough to stay at home with her younger siblings and even cook dinner for the family. She would have to stand up on a can in order to reach the stove, but that was okay. She loved doing her part – as long as it wasn't field work.

The house they lived in had been built for them by the landowner. It had four rooms: a living room, a kitchen, and two bedrooms. Right in the center was a wood-burning stove used for heat and for cooking. Since there was no running water, they would have to go to the well and dip the water for their usage. (And of course, their bathroom was an outside building).

Their house was close quarters for such a large family, but the Colemans were a happy bunch. God was blessing them with things which were impossible to buy with money. Love, laughter, and adequate provision were always a part of their lives.

Now getting back to the day at hand, Lottie was minding the children at the edge of the field. As the workers began working the closer rows, she could hear them singing the familiar hymns. She could also hear their conversation. "Did you see that, Ezera? Sarah almost got it last night!"

---

*God was blessing them with things which were impossible to buy with money.*

---

Got what? Why the Holy Spirit, of course. That's what life was all about. That's what the Coleman family lived and breathed for. There was a mighty awakening going on in North Mississippi, and their family was at the helm. Of course, they still worked in the fields so that they could buy their necessary provision, but the thrust of their lives was toward the church.

**The Church**

Since Pastor Coleman had taken over the reins, the three churches he led had thrived. There had been no black spirit-filled churches in North Mississippi prior to this, so news traveled fast, and many wanted to at least see what was going on.

Sundays were busy from the start. Ezera would sometimes get frustrated as she tried to comb everyone's hair. They didn't believe it was holy to use flatirons and rollers or to cut the hair, so it took lots of time and patience to get all of the tangles out. Then Pastor Hardy's shirt needed to be well pressed. Finally, everyone would be ready, and they would pile into their car.

As the family drove up to the school building where Booth's Chapel met, the yard would be full of white people. (This was not usually the way things happened in that day). Pastor Hardy would enter the building and take his place in the front of the church. Tremendous excitement would break out as he would deliver his message from the Bible. The white people would gather at the windows and listen, since there was no room for them inside. They too wanted to hear about God and His Spirit. They too wanted to receive His best.

Some people would come to the front and sit on the benches provided for those who wanted to receive the Holy Spirit. These benches were called "seekers' benches," and when people came and sat on them, they were signifying that they too wanted to receive the Holy Spirit. And many did. Many people were saved, healed, and delivered from the works of the devil.

After all of the singing, preaching, and praying, the service would be over. Then the family would pile into their Model A Ford, with diapers taped up to serve as windows, and head for home. It would be late, so several of the children would fall asleep. Ezera would have packed a few snacks for the children to eat on the way home. It would be dark in the back, so she would call their names one at a time. The ones who answered got a treat; the others must have been asleep.

---

*This business of ushering God' people into a deeper revelation of His Spirit and His Word was an all-consuming business.*

---

The ones who were awake would hear their dad excitedly sharing what had happened at church and what God had been showing him. Ezera would listen in silence, as her husband talked. They made a good pair – complementing each other.

Sometimes, as they traveled, the family would encounter someone stopped on the side of the road with car trouble. Pastor Coleman would never pass them by, regardless of the late hour or the fatigue he might be feeling. Someone needed help, and that would override everything else.

This business of ushering God' people into a deeper revelation of His Spirit and His Word was an all-consuming business. It required not just Pastor Coleman. It required the whole family. Of course, his wife, Ezera, was important to the mission, but so were the children.

Many Sundays would require a mid-afternoon meeting at someone's house. That was never as much fun, because usually there were no other children there. Besides, they were tired from the morning meeting. Yet, God's work came first, and everyone knew that. They knew that their father was tireless in his drive to see God's work done in North Mississippi.

Such were the days of the Coleman family. There was one mission, and everyone took part.

*The Lord shall increase you more and more, you and your children.*

*Psalms 115:14*

# 5

## Continuing On

S kipping ahead seven years, we see many changes in the Coleman family. Life goes on, and several more big events. They are still on the "path" we've talked about. The Colemans are on the righteous path, and regardless of what happens, God is always there for them.

The family has moved to Union County by now. When better opportunities had arisen, they had moved to several farms in Benton County before making this more extreme move. Moving to a different county also meant different schools for the children, so more adjustments than normal. They were still sharecropping, so the children still had to miss school on occasion in order to help with the fields.

Their biggest changes, however, had come in their family structure. Two more babies had been born during the last seven years. Dwight was born in 1953 and Mildred in 1956. Bobby was now about 15 and going through a teenage growth period. Lottie was 14 and still serving as undersecretary to her mother. Carnelia and Mary Ruth were 12 and 10 respectively. Hardy Jr. was 7. The family was not just growing larger in size; the children were also growing up. They were increasingly able to contribute to the welfare of the family and the churches.

The children each had their special slots in the family. Bobby was recognized as a leader, but Lottie was dubbed "Mother Goose," designated by her "bossier" role. Carnelia and Mary Ruth were the "Pretty One" and the "Comedienne," respectively. Hardy, Jr. (called Junior by the family) was the "Holy One."

Junior was developing into a remarkable young boy. As they worked in the fields, he could often be heard singing or shouting praises to God. Being the youngest working member of the family, Junior would be at the end of the row, and suddenly they would see his hoe rising in the air, high above the tall stalks of corn. The others would know that he was raising his hands in praise to God.

There was one evening when they were supposed to attend a church meeting, but the car wouldn't start. They tried everything, but to no avail. So everyone went back into the house, thinking that they wouldn't be able to go that night. Everyone, that is, except

Junior. As his older sisters looked out of the window, they saw the tiny silhouette of their little brother against the evening sky. He was kneeling at the bumper of the car, praying for God to get them to church.

And He did!

The older ones watched in amazement as some church members arrived to take them to the meeting. When the family didn't show up, they had decided to check out the situation. The prayer of faith was answered, even when it came from a small boy.

There was one time when Bobby had a terrific headache and turned to his much younger brother. "Come here, Red (that's what Bobby called his younger brother), and pray for me." He was astounded when the pain stopped. Junior's prayers were answered all right. Amazing!

---

*The prayer of faith was answered, even when it came from a small boy.*

---

Junior also spent some time fasting, as he diligently sought God. His mother would cover his plate and set it aside for later when he would be through praying. But food was scarce, and Carnelia was not going to let it be wasted. She would sneak into the kitchen and eat his dinner, much to Junior's chagrin – and much to hers when Junior got hold of her later!

That wasn't Carnelia's only sneaky trick. All of the girls were required to wear long skirts and to wear their hair up in buns as they attended school. Well, beautiful Carnelia wasn't satisfied with that rule, so as soon as she was in the school building, she would roll up her skirt at the waist to make it shorter. She would then let her hair down and shake it loose so that it would be down to her shoulders.

As her sisters passed her in the hall, they could hardly recognize her – and did they ever tell Daddy! Uh-oh. She was in trouble for sure!

With so much responsibility on his shoulders, it would have been easy for Pastor Hardy to let some of his children's discipline slide, but he didn't. Their well-being was the most important part of his life, and he demonstrated it many times.

As the children sat in church, they were like most children, in that sometimes they would talk and laugh at inappropriate times. So they would first get the "stare" from their Dad. As he sat on the podium, he would look directly at them in a way that they knew their behavior was being monitored. If they didn't take proper notice of that, he would wink at them, and then look down. Oh no! That was serious. They were going to get a spanking when they got home.

And he never forgot. Sometimes they would get the "wink" and try to avoid it by rushing to bed and pretending to be asleep, but to no avail. He would come in, and get them out of bed for their punishment. Pastor was a man of his word, and he was careful to fulfill all of his promises. "This hurts me worse than it hurts you," he would say. The correction they received showed them his love, and it instilled discipline into their lives.

There was one time when Mary Ruth (remember she was the comedienne), sitting on the second row at church, noticed a lady with a peculiar way of clapping her hands in praise. It was clear to Mary Ruth that this needed to be addressed, so she began to copy her – in a mocking way. Some of the children around snickered, as it was obvious that she was copying the lady. But then she looked up at her Dad and noticed she was getting "the stare."

The young girl had a choice. *Do I follow my Dad, or do I continue to entertain my friends?* she thought. Well, the latter won, and she raised her hands above her head to emphasize the mocking. - Wrong choice! Her dad left the platform and came down to Mary Ruth's side. As he took her hand and led her out of the sanctuary for her "talking to," she was very aware of the mistake in her decision. She would never again mock the worshipers, even if they seemed foolish to her.

Pastor Hardy was a disciplinarian, but the discipline was always born out of his love for his family. He wanted them to grow up knowing the wonderful God he served, and he wanted them to grow up with honorable attributes. Character, a good work ethic, as well as holiness.

There would often be times of family prayer. Dwight remembers how they would all gather to honor God and to petition Him for their needs.

At times, their provision would seem scarce, as in the times when they would have to coast down the hills on the way to church meetings, conserving gas in order to get there. And there were times when the houses in which they lived had tin over the windows, in order to keep out the cold winter air. There were also times when Pastor Hardy would go without an overcoat in winter in order for his children to have warmth. Yet always they would gather and praise God and learn to trust Him in all things. And over the years, the family would see their God come through for them in dramatic ways.

In the year 1958, you would hear some teenage talk from the older children in the household. "Daddy's too strict. He won't let me go to that party next weekend." "Some of my friends are wearing makeup and flat ironing their hair. Why can't I?" Yet you will also hear the reply of that virtuous woman, *who does her husband good and not evil all the days of her life, (Proverbs 31:12)* as

Ezera reminds them. "You know that your Daddy is a good man. He loves God and he loves you. Now you do what he says." If they complained about some requirements of their rigorous schedule, she would admonish them, "You know that everything that your Daddy does, he does for God."

Ezera was always showing respect for her husband and demanding it from the children. As they would be selfishly jockeying for position, she would say, "Now you know that the Word says that you are to *do unto others as you would have them do unto you.*" – Her calmness bringing order back into the atmosphere.

---

**Ezera was always showing respect for her husband and demanding it from the children.**

---

A few years later, Pastor Coleman built a house for his family in Blue Mountain, a few blocks away from his church, Flatwood Grove. It had  many modern conveniences – just as they had dreamed about. By then, Bobby and Lottie had left home, and Junior was soon to follow. Dwight and Mildred remember this well, because some of their childhood memories were from that place.

Dwight, being a typical big brother, loved to play pranks on Mildred. One time he pulled the circuit breaker in the house when just the two of them were there. Young Mildred was frustrated that none of the gadgets would work – and then she became afraid as night approached with no lights. When her father arrived, she was sitting outside just waiting for justice to be done. And she was not disappointed. (Probably Dwight was). He didn't even get the stare and the "wink" as he would have in church!

**Mary Ruth, Lottie, Carnelia, Junior, Dwight, and friends.**

The youngest two had a different field experience from the older children. Dwight has some memories of trying to short cut his responsibilities in the field – and getting in trouble again. Mildred really never made it to the field. Pastor Coleman stopped farming and began construction full time the year before she would have had to do it. Whew!

## Fast Forward: 2014

Fast forwarding to 2014, sitting at a table with all of the Coleman children – now with children and grandchildren of their own, it is obvious that God's hand has been upon their lives. Several of them indicate that there had been seasons of rebellion during their teen or young adult years, but God's word was like a yoke which had pulled them back to the truth of their Savior.

Today they are all walking with their Lord. Bobby went on to be with the Lord a few years ago, but was leading a congregation in Chicago when he died. Now Junior leads a congregation there, and the rest of the generations are peppered with ministers – all the way to the great-grandchildren. All of Bishop Hardy's children are actively involved in God's work in some capacity.

I ask, "What were the characteristics which caused your parents to be such great parents?" Of course, everyone echoes their faithfulness to God and to each other. "Our parents loved each other unconditionally. And they respected each other. There was never yelling in our home – at each other or at the children."

As for the children, their father would be kind – even in times of punishment. He would always explain why he was requiring certain things. And he took the time to explain how to do things even as they worked. (His training of Junior as a carpenter, always explaining the steps and the principles, set his son up to be a certified carpenter when he went to Chicago in his late teens).

"They were also totally real." There was no hypocrisy. They were at home the same way they were at church. They truly believed what they taught, and they expected others to believe it also.

## *They were totally real.*

Over the years, the children had seen some injustices perpetrated on their parents by landowners or others who were dishonest. One such was the last farm owner he had worked for, who was trying not to pay the agreed upon wage. Elder Hardy didn't argue or get into a fuss over it. He just walked up to the man's house and boldly declared, "Your mules are in the barn and your cotton is in the field." He then walked away and never returned to farming. That's when he entered the field of construction full time as a livelihood.

One of the things which his children respected the most about their father was that "he couldn't be stopped. He had a drive which surpassed any obstacle." When issues would arise in the church, he would meet the challenge. And the same would go for his home.

When his teenagers would seem rebellious, he would pray unceasingly. During one of these times, Elder Coleman put an empty chair in the front of the church for an absent son. He was demonstrating his faith that the son would eventually return to church – and return he has!

A remarkable man – and a remarkable family. All touched by God – and all showing the blessing showered upon a man and woman who were so faithful to Him.

*Thou therefore, my son, be strong in the grace that is in Christ Jesus.*

*2 Timothy 2:1*

# 6

# Change In the Church Scene

Just as the family had changed over the last few years, so had the church scene. By the half century mark, Pastor Hardy had turned over Perry's Chapel to another minister. He would go and preach there once in a while, but someone else was in charge. He was still the leader of Booth's Chapel and Bald Knob, both of which were continuing to grow.

It was a big job going from church to church – a distance of about 30 miles – in order to preach the Word. Then, of course, there were all of the needs of the congregants during the week. Sickness, family problems, and other needs would pop up. Needs which couldn't wait until Sunday.

In addition, not ever wanting to stand still, Pastor Coleman had started a new enterprise. He had bought a tent and had begun having tent meetings around the counties. There were many people who were afraid to go to church, so he would go to them. Maybe they felt condemned because of their lifestyles, or maybe they felt like their clothes weren't appropriate or they didn't have means of transportation. For whatever reason, there were some who didn't go to church, but who would turn to God under a tent. So he met that need.

It was during this season that Pastor Coleman joined another denomination. When he first came to the Lord, the church was a part of the Glorious Church of the Lord Jesus Christ, a holiness denomination which included just a handful of related churches. After a few years, the group split and had their members join two different groups. Some went to the Church of God and some went to the Church of God in Christ.

Both of these groups seemed solid, but there was lots of bickering among the church members and leaders as to which doctrine was the better. Not desiring to get into all of the fighting, Pastor Coleman stayed away from either one and remained independent for a season.

Pastor Coleman was an affable man, very compassionate toward the needs of his people and he would stop at nothing in order to meet those needs. Yet he was also a strong leader, and would not be pushed around by anyone. He exuded the authority of God.

One Sunday, during this nondenominational season, Pastor's authority got put to the test. A man walked into the church service with a fine suit and a big briefcase, signifying an authority of his own. He stood up in front of all the church members and began to rebuke Pastor Coleman. "All of the spirit-filled churches from here to the Louisiana line are under the leadership of my Bishop, and you need to bring your church under his leadership also."

Pastor Coleman, knowing the untruth of that statement and also knowing the selfish motives of this man, had a reply inspired by God. He stood up tall and bold as he declared, "The Constitution of the United States of America promises me the right to worship as I please, and I have no intentions of coming under that man's leadership." Embarrassed, the man with the briefcase quickly exited the church. He had gone from church to church, trying to con the people into joining his group. He was obviously looking for money, power, and stature.

Not this pastor. Hardy Coleman was no pushover.

The authority demonstrated that day was one of God's gifts which would again and again manifest in Pastor Coleman's life. That strength kept him on track when church members or leaders would cause trouble. That strength would also propel him forward to build new churches and undertake new endeavors. When he knew that God had spoken and he knew that he had heard

73

correctly, this man of God would take action, even if no one understood.

Pastor Coleman had been approached by another denomination for several years, but there was one item of their doctrine which bothered him. So he waited, and when that item was changed, he joined. In the late 60's Pastor Hardy joined The Church of The Living God, The Pillar and Ground of Truth. As he brought his churches under that umbrella, the presiding Bishop immediately made him a District Elder, with the oversight of several other congregations.

The Bishop could see the strength of this man of God and could see his energy and determination. Instead of stagnating, Pastor Coleman was getting things done for God's kingdom. He was a valuable asset to the denomination. And the denomination would prove to be a valuable asset to him.

---

*Some people watch things happen.*
*I like to make things happen.*

---

*Some people watch things happen; I like to make things happen.* This is the motto of Bishop Hardy Coleman, and it shows. As we look back over his years, we realize that there was always movement, and always progress.

For several years, Pastor Coleman traveled back and forth between Ashland and Blue Mountain, in order to instill the Word of God into the believers at Booth's Chapel and Bald Knob. At the time, the Bald Knob congregation was meeting in a school building on Hell Creek Road, just outside of Blue Mountain. As had always been the case, there was conflict between the doctrines of the holiness people and others. As a result, the trustees of the school board would sometimes take steps to close down the former. As a result, sometimes when Pastor Coleman would show up for church, the building would be locked.

Eventually, Elder Coleman came to the conclusion that they needed their own building, so he began praying for that. Some deacons at Bald Knob owned some property just outside of Blue Mountain, and they offered to help build a church building there. Elder Coleman was ready for it. This was a new day in the development of the church – to have their own building, and one which was designed to function as a church.

In 1952, Flatwood Grove Church was finished and the congregation from Bald Knob moved in for a renewed encounter with God. They were excited to have their own facility, and so was the pastor. Elder Hardy and Ezera would continue to lead that congregation, which would become the foundational thrust of every subsequent endeavor of the Colemans.

For 62 years, Hardy Coleman has been pastor of Flatwood Grove. As the years progressed, and new ventures would be undertaken, the Flatwood Grove congregation would be instrumental in helping. Sometimes busloads of believers from this church would travel to Ripley, Memphis, or Tupelo in order to bring revival to a new location. Members would serve in tents and in buildings, give offerings, provide music, lead worship, lead prayer, and share God's word. They have what's called the "whatever-it-takes" mentality – in order to help Bishop Coleman accomplish God's purpose.

---

*They have what's called the "whatever-it-takes" mentality.*

---

In the early 80's, a total renovation of the building was done. By this time, Elder Coleman had lots of experience in construction, so he led the project. A new sanctuary was added, as well as offices – to triple the square footage of the facility. At the same time, a new entrance, a steeple, and brickwork were added to complete the appearance.

Over the years, dozens of people have been called into ministry and launched from this church in the small town of Blue Mountain, Mississippi. In fact, this congregation has helped to change the entire area. Today this lively congregation includes several generations of some families – including Bishop Coleman's. His children, grandchildren, and great grandchildren help with the preaching, the music, and the youth ministry. The church is a testimony to the faithfulness of God to a man, when the man is faithful to Him.

*Her children arise up, and call her blessed; her husband also, and he praiseth her.*

*Proverbs 31:28*

# 7

# A Hard Farewell

During the next thirteen years, the ministry continued to blossom. Significant numbers were saved and healed, and many called to preach. The fire of God on Elder Coleman was contagious, and he helped dozens of young men and women find their own place in God, sending several ministers out to lead other congregations.

Flatwood Grove had continued to prosper, and tent revivals throughout Northeast Mississippi brought in new believers. People, even those with a different doctrine, were recognizing Elder Coleman as a powerful man of God.

The family certainly had changed during that time. Everybody had grown up, and most of the children had left home to start their own families. Dwight was the only one at home.

The livelihood had changed also. Though there were collections from the church, Elder Coleman still didn't count on those for their entire provision. He had purchased a store in Union County, and several in the family were helping to run that. As her children got older, Ezera had started to work as a nurse's assistant at the hospital in that county. And there was still the carpentry work... This family was a hard-working family.

Over the years, Ezera had developed something she called, "indigestion," which had caused her considerable discomfort from time to time. When Mildred was very young, this condition went on for several days, and even demanded bed rest for awhile. But in every incident the condition would pass, and Ezera would continue her business as usual.

During the Christmas season of 1976, things changed, however. Ezera had to have a hysterectomy, and as she was recovering, she just didn't seem the same. Mildred excitedly brought her a Christmas gift, knowing that her mother would be thrilled with her choice, but Ezera seemed almost indifferent. Usually her mother would pretend even more excitement than merited, but not this time. Having unwrapped it, she merely mumbled, "That's nice," and laid it aside. Mildred immediately recognized some distress with her mother. She just wasn't acting like herself.

Ignoring the need to rest, Ezera tried to go back to work. After all, this was the woman who had raised this large family, worked in the fields, cooked, cleaned, kept her husband in preacher-quality ironed shirts, worked in a hospital, and helped run the store – besides helping with the ministry. She felt invincible; this fatigue would pass.

But this time it was different.

**Ezera (right) with her twin sister, Rutera.**

While tending the family store, Ezera broke out into a cold sweat and almost fainted. It was obvious that their mother needed help, so Mildred and Lottie took her to the doctor and then to Elder Coleman's mother's house where she could receive prayer and necessary rest. She was very sick from what the doctor had diagnosed as "flu."

The family rushed to her side, immediately recognizing that her condition was very grave. Elder Coleman was concerned that Ezera wouldn't eat and wouldn't even take water. She was getting dehydrated. - They all agreed that it was time for the hospital.

An ambulance took Ezera to the hospital, and soon after she was admitted, she had cardiac arrest. The nurses were able to initiate defibrillation, and it started again. But not for long.

This precious woman of God, the one who had faithfully fulfilled her call as wife, mother, and grandmother, left the earth to spend eternity with Jesus. At only 56 years old, Ezera Starks Coleman had suffered a massive heart attack.

Shock and hysteria filled the room. Some of the children were so distraught, they had to have medical attention themselves. All of their lives, this woman had been incredibly strong for them all. She had represented God to her children when they couldn't hear for themselves. They just couldn't believe that she was gone!

This "suddenly" was too much to bear.

Elder Coleman was dazed and hurting as he went to his mother's house to stay. He didn't want to go home to his lonely house, it would only bring about pain. This loss was the greatest he had ever encountered, and it would take some time to recover from the shock.

I heard a minister say one time that when two people are married, they are like two plants planted in the same pot. The longer they stay in a good marriage, the more tightly their roots get entangled, and one can't be removed without disturbing the roots of the other. That's the way it was with Elder Coleman; his roots were truly disturbed.

Mildred and her husband moved in with her father so that he wouldn't be alone. All of the family worried about him. They had never seen such sadness on their father.

It was a time to mourn.

Mildred and her husband moved in with her father. They cooked, cleaned, and tried to continue with some of the tasks Ezera had mastered for their father. But Ezera was the master at providing her husband's needs, and her shoes were hard to fill.

Yet our God is a faithful God, and never would He leave His man in such great sorrow. God had a plan that would bring terrific comfort.

*Thou wilt shew me the path of life: in thy presence is fulness of joy; at thy right hand there are pleasures for evermore.*

*Psalms 16:11*

# 8

# New Blessings

I can still remember where I was standing when I received the phone call, Bishop Coleman will tell you. *What phone call*, you might ask? The one which would introduce him to his new bride, of course.

As one might expect, when this handsome, vibrant minister became available, the matchmakers came out in force. Everybody had a sister, or a neighbor, or a neighbor's friend who would be just perfect for Elder Coleman, so they thought… But not so fast. This man of God had spent his entire life serving the One who mattered, and he was not about to draw back now, or to link up with someone who didn't have the same motives.

This time the phone call was different. This time the call came from the daughter of the minister who had been Elder Coleman's mentor when he first received the Holy Spirit. This was a sanctified woman, one who understood the life of a set apart minister, and she had a cousin…

Excited, Elder Coleman immediately made an appointment to meet this recommended lady, and it didn't take long for God to speak and confirm that this was his new bride. The couple met at her home on February 21ˢᵗ, and they were married on the second day of April. (Do you remember that I said that there were many "suddenlies" in Elder Coleman's life? Well, here we go again).

So who was this new lady? What was so special about her? Many things were special, and you will see as we continue the story.

Annie Louise Lathon was born on a farm in Saltillo, Mississippi on July 11, 1927. She was the 5ᵗʰ child in a family which would eventually have 14 children. (8 girls and 6 boys). The Lathon family lived on a farm as sharecroppers, just as Elder Coleman's had, but they didn't move as often – only once. The farm on which they lived and worked was a large plantation, with about 10 homes clustered together for the workers, and a common well for all to share.

If we were to drop in on the Lathons during the 30's, we might be stymied by the activity. The great depression was going on, of course, and people were suffering and going without provision. But not this household. Oh, of course things were scarce, but the

Lathon family had an edge. They had a Proverbs 31 mother leading their charge, and her industrious ways could accomplish tasks that others could only dream about.

Mrs. Lathon's organization would make a best-selling magazine cover story today. Before going into the field to work with her husband, this mother would draw a line in the dirt in the backyard of their home. Then she would give clear instructions to the young

**Mrs. Lathon**

children who were staying at home to baby sit. "When the sunrays get to that line, I will be coming home soon, and it will be time to start dinner." So the children who were too young for the fields, but old enough to help with their younger siblings, would obediently watch out for the sun's position, and begin dinner accordingly.

There was much to do when Mrs. Lathon arrived home, so it was important for the schedule to be strictly adhered to. So what did she do when she returned home? There were many children to clothe, so she would get busy with her sewing. The girls would get out their "dream book," the Sears Roebuck Catalog, and pick out dresses. Then their mother would purchase some fabric from the "peddling truck" which regularly came by their house, and copy the dresses. She didn't need a purchased pattern; she could make one herself.

During the depression, sometimes fabric was scarce, so Mrs. Lathon would take worn out men's underwear to make stockings for the babies, and old felt hats to make their booties. A used adult coat would still have enough good fabric to cut down for a child's coat. Nothing went to waste. While others were moaning about how tough things were, Ann's mother didn't have time for that. She was making things work.

"My mother could make a meal out of anything," says Mother Ann. Not only did they have the fresh produce which was grown in their garden, but the children would be sent out to look for berries and plums. There would be immediate desserts, but also lots of canning. If she had no flour, she would use cornmeal, and if she had no sugar, she would use molasses. There was always a way to provide the needs of her family.

Ann remembers their Easter celebrations with great joy. Her mother would boil eggs and decorate them with crayons. Then she would hide them – again and again and again. Afraid that the dogs outside would eat the eggs before the children could find them, Mrs. Lathon would do all of the Easter egg hunts indoors. A coat pocket, a shoe box, or a pan in the kitchen might be the hiding place, as the children ran through the four rooms, laughing and pushing each other to get to the eggs first.

Outside of their home life, church was the most important activity for this family. All of the children would squeeze into their Model A Ford and start to church. Before they left home, their dresses would be starched and pressed to Mrs. Lathon's standards, but the crowded trip would override her efforts, and the dresses would be wrinkled by the time they arrived at their destination. Oh well, they made it, and that was the important thing. They had come to worship the Lord. They had also come to visit with friends and family – to share dinners on the ground, and to share the news of the day.

School was also important, but more of an effort. The children had to walk five miles one way to school, so they were tired when they arrived, and even more tired when they returned home. Mrs. Lathon would have fresh teacakes waiting for her children when they arrived, or Molasses bread. She was always looking out for their well-being.

Ann was a year behind in school because of a terrible accident. When six years old, she and her sister, Elnora, were vying for a special chair in front of their fireplace. As they were laughing and wrestling each other, the chair turned over and a black teakettle full of steam was knocked over on Ann's hand and arm, burning it severely. She was rushed to the doctor for treatment, but the healing was slow. There were many treatments to follow, and it took about a year for full recovery. During that time, Ann couldn't go to school, so she missed out on her start.

Remember the great dust storm of 1937 which came through young Hardy's territory? Well, it came through Saltillo as well. People had never seen anything like this, and they didn't really know what it was. There was a whirling wind carrying the dust in a tsunami-like wall, racing across the land. Ann was too young to work in the field, so she was taking care of the younger children at home while her mother tended the field, when this strange thing happened.

Frightened, the children felt that the safest place to be was their mother's bed, so they ran to her bed and covered up. They could see nothing – only yellowish dust whirling toward them, covering everything in its path.

Ann's mother, knowing that her younger children would be frightened, sent an older brother home to take care of them, but he couldn't make it. The wind was so strong, and the dust so powerful, that he had to stop and hold on to a wire fence for his safety. The children were left to fend for themselves. It was a scary moment in Saltillo, just as it had been in Benton County.

Safety, provision, work, fun, and laughter were all a part of Ann's growing years. As she reached adulthood, she was ready for her responsibilities of leading a large family. She not only knew how to cook and sew, but also to knit, quilt, crochet, and embroider. The only craft Ann's mother was hesitant to teach her children was the ability to make patches. (Mrs. Lathon wanted her girls to marry men who would provide well enough so that they wouldn't have to patch their clothes).

**Ann and her sisters**

## Holy Spirit Intervention

The Lathons often attended a church close to their home called Colom Chapel. It was a spirit-filled church, and frequently they held extended revival meetings. (The Holy Spirit revival which had hit Benton County had impacted Saltillo as well). Ann's mother was a devoted Christian, so any time some special revival meetings were being conducted, the family attended.

When Ann was 18 years old, an unusual thing happened. There were some services being held at Colom Chapel, and her family went. As usual. No great excitement in that. But tonight was different. One of Ann's friends, a girl who didn't seem to be particularly "religious," received the Holy Spirit, and she was obviously greatly affected by the experience. Recently, Ann had seen quite a few of the adults receive, but this was different. Suddenly, when Ann saw this friend receive, it provoked her. To see someone her own age filled with the Holy Spirit and speaking in tongues really impacted her. She wanted this gift also.

Ann couldn't sleep that night, and the next day at school she was disturbed all day, not even wanting to eat her lunch. This was too much to bear! Her friend had been blessed in this way, and she hadn't. *Well, tonight I will receive the Holy Ghost*, she thought.

So as Ann went to the meeting, she wasted no time in going to the front to sit on the "seekers bench." She really wanted this experience. The teenager sat and sat, and waited and waited, and not much happened. Then one of the leaders said, "Do we have any testimonies from the seekers' bench?"

Suddenly, Ann looked up and began to sing her reply. Not knowing why she was singing, since she had never sung in church before, Ann sang a new song, one which just flowed out of her: "If I live right, I'll overcome someday." Then she said, "Pray for me, that I may receive…" Ann meant to say, "the Holy Ghost," but she couldn't. She had already received. Suddenly a fluent prayer language in tongues came flowing from Ann. She prayed for a little while, and then seemed to doze off.

When her consciousness returned, the sight was amazing! The whole room was full of light. There were only two small light bulbs in the building, one over the congregation and one over the pulpit. So there wasn't much natural light, yet the whole room seemed full of light. Everyone looked different. Everything seemed so alive and glowing.

---

## *The whole room was full of light.*

---

Later, as Ann went home, everything still looked different to her: there was so much light everywhere! She looked in the mirror, and even her face was glowing! She had never experienced anything so powerful!

The next day, as she went to school, Ann still was having this experience of newness. She didn't kick that annoying cat out of the way as she left the house. And strangely, even the dirt in their yard, the dirt that was bothersome as they raked it, even that was beautiful. What a joyful experience!

A foundation was being laid for a holy life unto God. There would be obstacles ahead, and sometimes disappointments, but Ann's life would be a special one. As she walked with God, He would care for her and train her. She had a lot to do for her Lord, and that would manifest as she went along.

## Motherhood

Let's back up a little.

When Ann was about 14 years old, she had visited Red Oak Grove Church with her parents for a special Children's Day program. There were many gifted musicians in the churches around, and often they would get together to sing for each other. Well, this was one of those days, and Ann was in for a treat.

One by one, the groups sang, but there was one which caught her attention: the one which sang, "Twenty Four Elders On Their Knees." In this group was a handsome teenager about Ann's age. He did a really good job with the singing, and she loved the way he looked. (And he seemed to be looking at her also).

Soon after, there was another meeting, and again they "eyed" each other. But the third meeting was the charm. This young man boldly sat next to Ann, and pretending to fall asleep, his head fell over on her shoulder. This embarrassed Ann, but delighted her at the same time. It was getting close to time for Ann to start receiving her first beau.

Mrs. Lathon had even prepared for this occasion. Since they needed a proper sitting arrangement for the guests to visit, Ann's mother had recruited her son's ability with hammers and saws to cut down the headboard on an extra bed they had, and make a frame for a sofa. Then Mrs. Lathon's sewing skills came into play for the cotton-stuffed cushions. It was perfect for the purpose of proper visiting.

Both families seemed to be pleased with the attention between these two. They were good, industrious people, and they would make a great pair to raise a fine family.

So, in May of 1947, after several years of courting, Ann married her young sweetheart, Fattlis (Jack) Harris. Their first house was a tiny two room shotgun house right on the farm. It was perfect for the two young lovers as they started out. They worked in the fields, and when Jack got his paycheck, he always brought his new bride a Payday candy bar – her favorite.

After a short while Ann's uncle built the couple a new house. It was still a two room shotgun house, but newer and nicer than before. After all, a kitchen and a bedroom were all they needed.

Several years and three babies later, a new opportunity came to Jack, but one which would require the two to move. Many of Ann's siblings were moving away from Mississippi so that they could have better opportunities. Her sisters were moving away to California, Chicago, Milwaukee, and Toledo. Since Jack was his mother's only son, he didn't want to move too far away, so they settled on Memphis. And when he discovered a job opening at a foundry in Memphis, Jack took it. Ann was pregnant with her fourth child, Elaine, as they made the move: a move which would allow Ann to stay at home and raise her children, an opportunity she relished.

Eventually, Ann would know why God was keeping her close to Mississippi. She was in the right place, for sure.

*New Blessings*

*As arrows are in the hand of a mighty man; so are children of the youth.*

*Psalms 127:4*

# 9

## A Family Grows In Memphis

Have you ever heard of the Harris Fortress on King Road in Memphis? Probably not. But it was there, and famous among the families in the neighborhood. Jack Harris had not only fenced in the backyard, but he had also planted a hedge across the front of the house. He was going to make certain that his four beautiful daughters were safe!

Jack and Ann Harris eventually had 7 children, and Ann was delighted to take on that responsibility. Annell and Louise had been born in Mississippi. Hoyal had also been born there, but had died at only three weeks, a sad time for the young mother and father. So they were happy that soon after, Ann was pregnant again. Elaine, Linda, Dennis, and Jerry were born in Memphis, and their family was complete.

Jack provided well for his family, and Ann employed all of the skills she had learned from her mother as she cared for her lively bunch. (In fact, Ann enjoyed the childcare so much, she eventually established a small daycare in her home).

So with the fortress they were safe, but that didn't mean that the Harrises weren't friendly. There was a Chinaberry Tree in the front yard – shaped like a large umbrella, and all of the neighborhood children and teens knew that they were welcome there. No grass could grow under that tree because of all of the activity. But that didn't matter. The children were safe and happy, and so were the parents.

While Bishop Coleman's children were growing up in Mississippi, Ann's children were growing up in Memphis. Both families had godly parents, and both families thrived as they grew.

Ann was an exceptional homemaker, and kept the fires of hospitality going for her family. She cooked a variety of meals during the week, but on Sundays the menu was always the same. Fried chicken, corn, mashed potatoes, English peas, and rolls. One Sunday, she decided to vary the menu to avoid boredom, so she cooked greens instead of peas. Everyone was shocked! They knew what to expect, and this was not it. There was such an uproar that she never varied the Sunday menu again.

The Harrises had other routines besides their Sunday menu. They knew that they were to be faithful in going to school and in doing their homework. They also knew that they would be faithful to their church.

**Jack and Ann Harris**

Jack had been raised in the Methodist Church, and wanted to continue in that tradition, so he would take the older children with him and Ann would take the younger ones as she attended a spirit-filled congregation. Of course, the church experiences were very different, the Methodist experience being very formal and quiet; the spirit-filled experience exuding noise and animation.

When the oldest daughters were young teenagers, Jack decided that all of the children should go together, so he agreed for them to go with their mother. That was quite an adjustment! The girls, who had been accustomed to quiet, formal services, had a hard time adjusting to the seemingly unruly behavior in the spirit-filled congregation.

Yet they did their best, and even organized a singing group, The Harris Sisters. They also joined the Bethlehem Jewels, another singing group. And they began to settle into the new traditions available.

Ann was well known in the church for her faithfulness. The pastor had a large family, and few resources for provision, so church members would have a "pounding Sunday," and bring food to help them out. Determined to provide for her leaders, Ann would make snowballs and candy apples to sell around the neighborhood in order to purchase food for the pastor's family. She would notice sales, loading her freezer for the big day. Thus Ann became well-known as the "Pound Queen."

*Ann was an exceptional homemaker, and kept the fires of hospitality going for her family.*

At home Ann taught her children to be obedient and diligent. She would look for talents in her children and help to develop them. One day, as Ann was cooking dinner and the younger ones were in the kitchen with her, Elaine looked up at the cabinet and said, "Morton's Salt." Surprised, Ann knew that her four year old daughter had read the words on the salt box, so she whipped into action. Obviously Elaine was exceptionally bright if she was reading at four, so Ann enrolled her in a preschool which would encourage that development. Of course, she was going to have to sell more candy apples and snowballs, but what of it? Her children were her greatest gifts from God, and she was going to honor Him by doing her best for them.

Later, when Elaine was ready for college, Ann continued to make extra money in order to send her. Her daughter was the first one in the family to go to college, but this was important. Her mind needed to be developed. As she graduated from Memphis State University, she began a career in education. (Today Elaine has just retired from a career as a school teacher and school administrator. All of that education paid off).

---

*Her children were her greatest gifts from God, and she was going to honor Him by doing her best for them.*

---

There were also piano lessons for Louise and Elaine. It was impossible to pay for two people, so Ann paid for one lesson, and the girls would take turns attending. Since there was no piano at home for practice, they would sit at the coffee table and work their fingers, pretending that a piano was there. In the end, they both learned to play, and both of them enjoy the piano today.

Though Ann was a first class nurturer, she also was a disciplinarian. Never were the children allowed to let their requirements slide. And since the house on King Road didn't have the right quality of switches, Ann would pick some from her mother's Saltillo home and bring them back to her freezer in Memphis. When actions required it, just the right amount of "ouch" would be available to drive home a point.

**Jerry and Dennis Harris**

With a house full of bright, lively youngsters, Ann had to stay on her toes. And that she did! Louise insists that her mother was the originator of the "Stand Your Ground" law, though Ann's version had a little different twist. Ann always wanted her children to stay indoors when she had to go to the store or run an errand. Safety first, you know.

One day, Ann left for an errand with the usual charge: "Lock the door behind me, and don't go out this door until I get back." A few minutes later, a boy from the neighborhood came by and waited under the Chinaberry Tree for the girls to come out and talk to him. Louise got antsy… She *really* wanted to go out, so she had a brilliant idea. She would be obedient. She would not go out the door; she would go out the window!

Although Louise was having a ball, her siblings could hardly wait for their mother to return and find out what their sister had done. She was going to get into trouble! And she did!

**Louise, Linda, Annell, and Elaine Harris**

Louise tried to finagle out of her dilemma by reciting the letter of the law, but to no avail. Her mother "stood her ground," and Louise's "loophole" had no bearing. Ann was not to be outsmarted by a heart of rebellion!

Sometimes, as with all teens growing up, the Harris youngsters would be annoyed with the rules. Many of their friends weren't as guarded by their parents, and they would be out late, running up and down the street, playing and visiting...and sometimes getting into trouble. During those years a public service TV ad came out which said, "It's 10 o'clock. Do you know where your children are?" Sitting in front of the TV set, all of the Harrises would roll their eyes and reply sarcastically, "Yes. Our Mother knows where we are!"

Occasionally, the teen within would rise up, and Annell and Louise would yield to temptation. They were only allowed to listen to Christian music, but they had a plan of their own. As their mother left for a trip to town, they would turn on the radio and listen to rock and roll (the Devil's music). They would hold onto the doorknobs, pretending they had partners. And the waxed floors would allow their sock feet to slide gracefully – giving an extra shine to the floors in the process. Just as she was returning, they would turn the radio back to Gospel, acting very pious.

Inwardly, the Harris children knew that the attention and discipline they received were all born out of a heart of love for them. They were very thankful for that love and care. They had an extraordinary mother, and she was establishing foundations of lives well lived – for Jesus and for their families.

Ann Harris had led, not only by her words, but by her deeds. She had led by example. They noticed as she prayed, or helped the sick and needy, or sold her wares in order to provide extra money for the church or for her children's interests. They noticed as she walked – in rain or cold – to Ford Road Elementary School, in order to cast her vote during elections.

Ann also led by incredible wisdom which, she shared. When there would be arguments, she would say, "When there's fire, someone has to be the water to put it out." And she would often be that water – a calm, quieting voice in the midst of the noise.

Ann Harris was an extraordinary woman.

*The path of life leads upward*
*for the wise*

*Proverbs 15:24 (NASB)*

# 10

## A New Era Begins

On July 11, 1975, the Harrises had been married for 28 years and had shared many joys and sorrows. They had raised six children, and helped many others. Ann had also been a faithful wife. The last decade had seen Jack's health wane and he had come to need increasing care. Being the kind of person she was, Ann faithfully and lovingly provided whatever care he needed.

This day was different, as he was now lying in a VA hospital. Ann went to see him and fed him his breakfast, noticing that he was very weak. Then, just as she returned home for a rest, she got the news: Jack had passed on to be with the Lord. He had been a good provider, and a faithful husband. Now he was gone.

The children gathered around Ann to mourn with her. They were all glad to see their father's suffering come to an end, for he had been ill for about 10 years. Yet it was hard to see their family lose their father. A chapter had ended in their lives.

Ann was only 48 years old when Jack died. Her children were around, and there were grandchildren as well, but she was a vibrant, healthy, beautiful young woman, and people began encouraging her to look for a new husband.

After a certain amount of grieving, Ann decided maybe that is what she wanted also, and as with anything in her life, Ann prayed for God's will. As she began to pray for a new husband, she said, "Father, I have been faithful to care for my husband in his sickness, now I'm asking for one of your best. I only want one of your best."

If you talk to Ann now, she will say that when you are young, you don't understand many things about life, and you just marry someone because of love for them. But when you marry in your middle years, things are different. There are so many people affected by your decisions. You have children and grandchildren, and you must consider them in any big decisions you make.

With this kind of awe concerning the possibility of marrying again, Ann said, "Father, let me know when it is the right one. Don't let me make a mistake."

When the phone call came from her cousin in Toledo, telling her about Elder Coleman, Ann felt excitement.

Her cousin said, "There is a man in Mississippi who lost his wife. He's a good man, and I think you should meet him." So Ann agreed, and a meeting was set up.

She dug in deeper on her prayers, reminding God that He must let her know if this man is for her. At this stage in her life, she didn't want to marry a man who wouldn't be a good father to her children and grandfather to her grandchildren. She also wanted to make sure that they would be able to minister to others together.

On February 21, Ann felt excitement and uneasiness at the same time. "Lord, let me know," she continued. The hour came and Elder Coleman arrived. Ann was putting on the finishing touches of her outfit, as her daughter let the Elder in, and seated him in the living room. Louise had tried to arrange a "grand entrance" for her mother, so she was there to open the door and greet the new suitor. Rushing to the back, Louise said, "Mother, I like him!"

---

*God was answering her prayer, and giving her the signal of approval by His obvious presence.*

---

When Ann walked out into the living room, her answer came immediately. To hear her describe it, she felt a halo of God's presence hover around her. It enveloped her head and shoulders, and she began to shake a little. God was answering her prayer, and giving her the signal of approval by His obvious presence. The two had not even engaged in any conversation yet, but Ann knew that Elder Coleman was "the one." A few weeks later, when Elder Coleman popped the question, Ann had only one reservation. Remembering her younger days in Mississippi, she asked, "Do you have indoor plumbing?" His affirmative answer sealed the deal.

On April 2, 1977, Ann Harris became first lady to Elder Coleman. Louise's house was the location for the event, as all of the children and grandchildren huddled around to celebrate. They knew that this was God's plan, and all of their children – 13 at the time, along with their spouses, and their many grandchildren, were happy to see their parents make the commitment. They had both been outstanding, devoted parents, and the two seemed very well suited.

Even Jerry, Ann's baby boy, had to admit this was the right thing, though at first he had had some reservations about losing his mother's cooking.

God's hand was blessing these two faithful ones in a new and significant way. All of the children were now out on their own, and more of Mother Ann's time, as well as Elder Coleman's could be devoted to God's work. Back in Mississippi, they continued to lead Flatwood Grove Church and to hold frequent tent meetings throughout the area. But this was just the beginning for God's new power team.

When you meet with Mother Ann, you know that you are in the presence of God. Her love, her faith, and her gentle spirit reach out to others, especially to her husband and her family. She is constantly encouraging and building up those around her - extending His love to others.

During the last few years, two of Mother Ann's children, Annell and Dennis, have gone on to be with the Lord. Annell from cancer, and Dennis from an accident during the writing of this book. The day after the accident, my husband and I went to her house to show our support.

Of course, there was sadness, but you could tell that Mother Ann was operating from another realm. Her serenity could only have come from that place of trusting in God - that secret place.

She continually knows how to cast her cares upon the Lord, and His faithfulness to her is evident.

*He who finds a good wife, obtains favor from the Lord. (Proverbs 18:22)* You can certainly see this in the life of the Colemans.

**Coleman Family Gathering.**

**Hardy with daughters.**

Elder Hardy and Mother Ann in Chicago.

The Global Pacific Diocese Elders 2014

Bobby and Mae Lee Coleman

Annell Brown

Dennis Harris

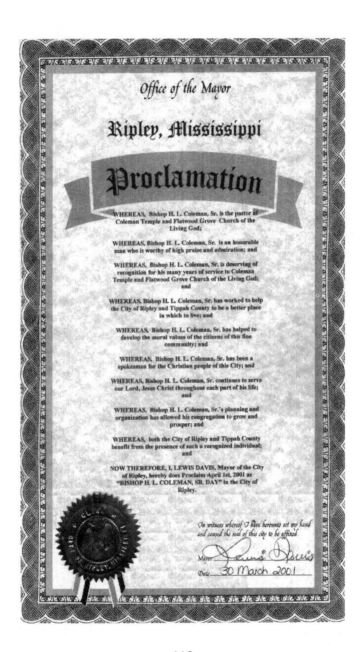

*Office of the Mayor*

# Ripley, Mississippi

# Proclamation

WHEREAS, Bishop H. L. Coleman, Sr. is the pastor of Coleman Temple and Flatwood Grove Church of the Living God;

WHEREAS, Bishop H. L. Coleman, Sr. is an honorable man who is worthy of high praise and admiration; and

WHEREAS, Bishop H. L. Coleman, Sr. is deserving of recognition for his many years of service to Coleman Temple and Flatwood Grove Church of the Living God; and

WHEREAS, Bishop H. L. Coleman, Sr. has worked to help the City of Ripley and Tippah County to be a better place in which to live; and

WHEREAS, Bishop H. L. Coleman, Sr. has helped to develop the moral values of the citizens of this fine community; and

WHEREAS, Bishop H. L. Coleman, Sr. has been a spokesman for the Christian people of this City; and

WHEREAS, Bishop H. L. Coleman, Sr. continues to serve our Lord, Jesus Christ throughout each part of his life; and

WHEREAS, Bishop H. L. Coleman, Sr.'s planning and organization has allowed his congregation to grow and prosper; and

WHEREAS, both the City of Ripley and Tippah County benefit from the presence of such a recognized individual; and

NOW THEREFORE, I, LEWIS DAVIS, Mayor of the City of Ripley, hereby does Proclaim April 1st, 2001 as "BISHOP H. L. COLEMAN, SR. DAY" in the City of Ripley.

*In witness whereof I have hereunto set my hand and caused the seal of this city to be affixed*

Mayor _____

Date _30 March 2001_

WHEREAS, Bishop H. L. Coleman, Sr. is the pastor of Coleman Temple and Flatwood Grove Church of the Living God;

WHEREAS, Bishop H. L. Coleman, Sr. is an honorable man who is worthy of high praise and admiration; and

WHEREAS, Bishop H. L. Coleman, Sr. is deserving of recognition for his many years of service to Coleman Temple and Flatwood Grove Church of the Living God; and

WHEREAS, Bishop H. L. Coleman, Sr. has worked to help the City of Ripley and Tippah County to be a better place in which to live; and

WHEREAS, Bishop H. L. Coleman, Sr. has helped to develop the moral values of the citizens of this fine community; and

WHEREAS, Bishop H. L. Coleman, Sr. has been a spokesman for the Christian people of this City; and

WHEREAS, Bishop H. L. Coleman, Sr. continues to serve our Lord, Jesus Christ throughout each part of his life; and

WHEREAS, Bishop H. L. Coleman, Sr.'s planning and organization has allowed his congregation to grow and prosper; and

WHEREAS, both the City of Ripley and Tippah County benefit from the presence of such a recognized individual; and

NOW THEREFORE, I, LEWIS DAVIS, Mayor of the City of Ripley, hereby does Proclaim April 1st, 2001 as "BISHOP H. L. COLEMAN, SR. DAY" in the City of Ripley.

*The steps of a good man are ordered by the LORD: and he delighteth in his way.*

*Psalms 37:23*

# 11

## Coleman Temple

After only a year of marriage, the one who "makes things happen," had a new vision. Noticing that there was no black spirit-filled church in Ripley nearby, Elder Coleman felt that he and Mother Ann, as she now was called, should start one. Very quickly, Ann showed her faith in God - and her husband, when she decided to throw in all of her savings which she had brought with her to the marriage. She took her $6,000, threw it into the pot, and the couple started on the first of what would be many endeavors together. They started Coleman Temple in Ripley, the Spirit-filled church they had dreamed about.

First they had to secure a location and purchase some land. After much deliberation, the Colemans decided on a plot in the worst section of town. Most people were afraid to go there because of the drug dealers and gangs. In fact, many tried to talk them out of that location. A church would be out of place in that area, many thought.

The nay-sayers didn't know that a rough area was exactly where Elder Coleman wanted his church to be. He wanted to minister to the drug addicts, the drug dealers, and others far from God. So they purchased a lot from a lady in the area, and began this new venture. In Mother Ann's words, "It looked like a wilderness, but we knew the vision was from God, so we pressed on."

They continued to seek God for wisdom and to pray that He would order their steps and guide them through the plan. With his wife by his side, Elder Coleman began the work. They had held many tent revivals in Ripley, and Elder Coleman knew that they were following God's plan.

However, things got off to a rocky start. It was very hot and dry, and the ground needed a lot of work to prepare for building, but that didn't stop the Elder. Then he developed an ulcer and started spitting up blood as he worked, but that didn't stop him. The devil began to mock him, telling him that he would never live to see it finished, but that didn't stop him either. Elder Coleman was determined that he was going to fulfill God's will in this place, and nothing could stop him.

They hauled in crossties for foundation, and bought some lumber, and one friend showed up to help with the building. After a hard day of putting up studs and laying beams, a strong wind came through that night, and the structure fell to the ground, shocking the workers as they arrived the next day. It didn't help that they had to suffer the laughter of the neighborhood children who said, "Preacher's church fall down. Preacher's church fall down." Neither did it help to hear the adults in the vicinity who came by to mock the work - not wanting a church nearby.

Yet the Colemans would not be stopped. Sometimes it takes determination to accomplish God's work, and they were definitely determined. The Elder was like Nehemiah. "I'm doing a good work, and I won't come down." With his one friend by his side, they worked...and worked...and worked.

As time rolled on, the hot, dry weather turned into the cold of winter, and their hands and faces felt the chapping of the icy wind. Now it was almost impossible to work, so they brought in a kerosene heater with a blower...and they continued. By this time, interest was aroused in a few others, and they, too, joined in with helping hands. Seeing that this project was going forth regardless of the obstacles, they wanted to be a part of it.

But there were also the mockers. Young people on drugs would stop by, cursing and laughing at the builders. It was obvious that the devil was threatened by this holy man who had come into his territory.

When the building was up enough to hold a service, others saw the progress and began to donate items. Someone brought some theater chairs. Ann varnished them, and painted the restrooms. One minister donated used carpet. Another brought in a heater that looked like a big hornet's nest, but it kept everyone warm. Black tar paper was put up around the structure to provide more warmth. It wasn't complete yet, but they could hold services.

They still needed more money to complete the project, so family and friends pitched in. Ann and Elder's mother baked cakes and pickles to sell. Ann's son-in-law located a business in Memphis which specialized in fund-raising candy, so he brought her some to sell. Then other ministers provided programs to help raise money. They brought in $100 at one and $80 at another.

Services continued with members from Flatwood Grove driving over to attend. There were no members of this new church for an entire year. The offerings would be as high as $55 sometimes, but never as high as $100 during the entire first year. But the Colemans were happy about their venture. They knew that God had told them to do it, and it would succeed. Ann describes it as feeling like a sitting hen: the egg was about to develop, and she knew it!

Close to the end of the first year, Ann began to have the same feeling she had felt when she first met Elder Coleman. The hovering of God's presence was with her, and she knew that something was about to happen.

Shortly after, they held an 8 week revival with Bishop Parks presiding. That was just the boost they needed. Many souls were saved and many received the baptism in the Holy Spirit. Drug dealers came to the Lord, along with addicts and others. Perseverance was paying off, and God's plan was coming to fruition. The church now had members, and they were on their way.

Coleman Temple began to be known as The Little Church with a Big Heart, a very fitting title for its mission. The big heart was the heart of God – looking through the sin and drawing the hearts of the people to their Creator. This church eventually developed several outstanding ministers. The current pastor, Elder Jeremiah Simmons, was one of the first converts. He is now an on-fire man of God, and a leader of several churches around.

*"Where sin abounds, grace does much more abound."* Romans *5:20.* Coleman Temple has demonstrated this Word.

Eventually, Coleman Temple began to televise their church services so that people at home could experience God's love. People all over north Mississippi could see God's power and His purpose, and many more came to the Lord as a result. Once more, Elder Coleman and Mother Ann had pressed forward – not just for the status quo, but for God's excellence.

---

## The hovering of God's presence was there and something was about to happen.

---

The work of Coleman Temple in Ripley was so significant that the Aldermen named the street after the Elder. Coleman Street is now where the church resides. And the impact on the city has continued to be so great that the mayor designated a Bishop Hardy Lee Coleman, Sr. Day in his honor – held on the first day of April of each year. It's a day honoring the man who has brought such profound change to the lives of the people of Ripley.

From Coleman Temple, many ministers have been raised up to take other churches. And countless people have had their lives transformed. Very few black people in the area haven't had a touch from Elder Coleman or Mother Ann as they passed through some tough times in their lives.

His influence has been transformational for the community.

*The Lord shall increase you more and more, you and your children.*

*Psalms 115:14*

# 12

## Keep On Pressing On

Things were humming along for Elder Coleman's Flatwood Grove in Blue Mountain and Coleman Temple in Ripley, and their tent revivals were continuing throughout the area. As always with churches, there were volatile episodes with people and their needs, so the Colemans had to work hard. Yet, as always with Elder Coleman and Mother Ann, as soon as they were able to handle what was at hand, they would reach for more. They didn't want ever to settle for less than what God wanted.

It was about this time that they became aware of a need in Memphis. Linda and Carey Williams and Annell and Marion Brown (two of Mother Ann's daughters and sons-in-law) had begun a Bible study in their home, and had invited others to join. Realizing that Carey was an elder and Marion was a deacon, they decided it was time to take the ministry to the next level. They noticed a one-room building which had been a church at one time, so they rented it to begin the new work, naming it after the street it was on, Mount Olive Street.

For a year they held services without any new members. The work came under the leadership of Elder Coleman, and he began to assist them by coming to preach every third Sunday, bringing with him a school bus full of worshipers to help out. At the end of the first year, they held some revival services in the front yard, drawing attention from their neighbors. That proved a turning point for Mount Olive, as many got saved and filled with the Spirit. They were on their way.

People began to come to the little building to see what was happening. There were healings and salvations – and lots of praise. There would be times when the floor in the building would shake so much from the jumping and shouting, that the deacons would have to gather outside and watch the foundation to make sure it wasn't caving in. After all, this was a small, primitive building, and the crowd was growing.

It was time for a change. As Linda was driving down Tchulahoma Avenue one day, she noticed a beautiful church building for sale. There was a huge piece of property with a magnificent brick building, parking lot, and youth building - well landscaped and ready for a congregation. At first it seemed foolish to even inquire, because obviously the facility was worth much more than they could afford. Yet knowing her God the way she did, Linda decided to check it out anyway.

The church which had been in that facility was closing, and they were planning to give the majority of the value to another congregation. There were some debts which had to be paid, but they were asking much less than it was worth.

---

## These people really meant business for God!

---

Two other church groups had applied for the building, so Linda sat down to write a letter explaining the desire of Mount Olive Church. She allowed the Holy Spirit to dictate as she wrote about the needs of the congregation and their vision for the future of the church. It was a stretch to think that they could come up with the necessary funds, but these leaders were trusting in God.

To their delight, and some surprise, the Mount Olive congregation was chosen to receive the property. (Later, Linda was told that her letter had been the tie-breaker. Her passionate vision had convinced the prior owners that the building would be placed into great service). Now the task at hand was to gather the funds necessary for the purchase. So as usual, Elder Coleman stepped up to the challenge. He was able to take $2,000 from his own bank account and borrow $2,000 from a friend. Yet the bank wanted more equity from the congregation to secure the loan, so Mother Ann's daughter, Louise Harris and James and Margie Burse put up the equity in their homes to accomplish the purchase. These people really meant business for God!

For several years Mount Olive was under the direct leadership of Elder Coleman. He was the presiding pastor overseeing the operations of Mount Olive, as well as Coleman Temple and Flatwood Grove. Quite an undertaking – with all of the traveling and so many different congregations.

When you ask Bishop Coleman today about lessons he learned along the way, he will quickly tell you, "You can't lead three congregations." The responsibility was too much – especially with the distance involved. So he turned over the leadership to a pastor who could be on top of the day to day operations.

Today Mount Olive is thriving under the leadership of Elder Terry Macon, a distant cousin of Bishop

Coleman. Still under the Diocese of Bishop Coleman, this Memphis congregation continues to reach for God's best.

*Though thy beginning was small, yet thy latter end should greatly increase.*

*Job 8:7*

# 13

## Reaching The Pinnacle

How does a son of a sharecropper, born in a small log cabin in a poor rural area, come to have an impact on an entire region? Where does he get the drive? The energy? The wisdom? And what makes him so successful?

The answers have many facets, but the source of each of them is God Himself. Hardy Lee Coleman, Sr turned his life over to his Creator at a very early age – and spent his entire life living out God's plan. Just as a giant Oak Tree grows and spreads its branches one inch at a time – and one year at a time, so Elder Hardy in following God, grew bit by bit and year by year. As he grew, his roots went deeper, his branches spread out over greater territory – and his influence stretched far beyond his wildest dreams.

In the year 2000, the greatest honor- and responsibility-he had ever encountered came to this unusual man.

Ever since Elder Hardy had come into the Church of the Living God, he had been a District Elder. That meant that he had been charged with the responsibility of overseeing several churches – besides the ones he had personally started. In fulfilling that mission, he had counseled and encouraged the pastors and helped to teach and inspire their members.

The Presiding Bishop over the Mississippi/Tennessee Region was Bishop Ollie Robins - a dedicated leader, who had led many congregations to greater heights. Toward the end of the 20th century, his health started to wane, and the Bishop knew that it was time to recommend a replacement.

Throughout his tenure in the denomination, Elder Coleman had demonstrated incredible leadership. Remember his motto? "Some people like to *watch* things happen; I like to *make* things happen." Well, he had given clear evidence of this belief as he had built churches, led others, and held tent meetings all around north Mississippi and into Tennessee. By this time, two of his sons had churches they were building in Chicago, and one of Mother

Ann's daughters and sons-in-law were starting a church in an Atlanta suburb.

Elder Coleman was an obvious choice as a recommendation for a bishopric. Since Elder Coleman already had so many churches under his oversight, the Church of the Living God leadership designated two men to take over for Bishop Robins: Elder Hardy Coleman and Elder G.T. Howell. So on October 20, 2000 at the 71st General Assembly of The Church Of The Living God, Elder Coleman was consecrated to the Bishopric. To be chosen for such a high level of authority in this denomination with churches all over the United States and even into foreign countries, was a huge promotion.

Bishop Coleman quickly met with his board, and began to plot out a new direction. They named their diocese the Global Pacific Diocese, with churches in Mississippi, Tennessee, Illinois, and Georgia. Elder

Henry Jeans was named State Elder for Mississippi, Elder Hardy Lee Coleman, Jr. was named State Elder for Illinois, and Minister Annette Gray was named State Secretary for Mississippi.

Now, enough of all that honor and recognition, it was time to get to work.

A considerable sum of money was in trust for the two new dioceses, and they divided that up. Bishop Coleman knew what he wanted to do with his cash. The diocese needed a large facility in which to hold state meetings, so he planned another building.

---

*Now, enough of all that honor and recognition, it was time to get to work.*

---

First the Bishop purchased the land from the former diocese – a plot in Tupelo, and he began securing plans and making big decisions. An Apostolic church was being erected near New Albany, Mississippi, and Bishop Coleman liked the overall effect. So he took those blueprints and modified them for his own endeavor. First, he had to hire someone to do the framework for the metal building, and then he lined up friends and other members to help him finish the work.

Mother Ann says that Bishop would lie in bed at night with his eyes open, praying. She would say, "What are you planning now?" He would give her a description which had come to him – from God, and every detail was eventually included. Beautiful columns and a portico on the front. Two mosaic tile crosses on the floor of the vestibule as you enter through the huge double doors. Arched doorways going into the sanctuary. The pulpit and the choir stand flanked with a mantle and wall columns. He also added a balcony, carpet, padded chairs, and furnishings to complete the

**Bishop Hardy with Elders. L-R Ray Jackson, Troy Starks, Hardy Coleman, Wyles Starks**

elegant surroundings. When it was finished, the sanctuary and balcony could seat close to a thousand people.

Six days a week for more than seven months, Bishop Coleman traveled from Blue Mountain to Tupelo (a roundtrip of about 80 miles), to work on the building. Oh, and by the way, Bishop was 82 years old at the time. He had already had heart bypass surgery, but he had recovered, and was determined once again not to be stopped. All of his work – and even the transportation costs – were gratis. Bishop's heart was, as usual, for the people and his own needs took a back seat.

Today the Global Pacific Diocese churches which are close by, meet every fifth Sunday at the Bishop H.L. Coleman Convention Center in Tupelo. Once a year, there is a national week-long meeting at the facility – drawing the people from Illinois and Georgia – as well as Mississippi and Tennessee.

As you look around the facility while a meeting is in full swing, there's energy everywhere, with people of all ages – from great-grandparents to tiny children – clapping their hands and praising their God. If you talk to anyone there, you will hear raves about their leader. He prayed for their healing, or he preached the sermon which caused them to turn their lives around, or he visited their mother, or he gave them some money when they needed it , or…the list goes on and on.

Though he has reached the pinnacle of success in his denomination, Bishop Coleman is a humble man whose desire is always for the good of others. His favorite story is still the one about his salvation – when he, as a young farm boy in overalls –met Jesus and received the baptism in the Holy Spirit.

All of the other stuff is just what happens to a man who truly follows his Creator.

*God also bearing them witness, both with signs and wonders, and with divers miracles, and gifts of the Holy Ghost, according to his own will?*

*Hebrews 2:4*

# 14

## Miracles in Mississippi

There have been many people who have joined with Bishop Coleman, helping him to fulfill God's call, but one stands out significantly, and that is his mother. Do you remember the account of the night young Hardy received the Holy Spirit? He had seen his mother go forward for healing just before he went to the front. Well that story needs some elaboration.

Willer Timsy Davis Coleman and her son, Hardy, were very close - especially since his dad had left and just the two of them were together at home. From the time that he was twelve years old, he had done all that he could to provide for the two of them — and she had taken a job as a housekeeper in order to bring in additional income.

The night Willer went forward for healing, she had a problem which Hardy hadn't known about- a tumor - and she was very concerned that it could be cancerous. That night was eventful in many ways. When she went up for Pastor Rapier to pray for her healing, she received total healing – and the tumor disappeared. At the same time, she also received the baptism in the Holy Spirit and a life change of her own.

When 18 year old Hardy Coleman and his mother went home that night, they both had been impacted – forever. As Willer grew in the Lord, she felt a calling to the healing ministry. She had freely received, and she was compelled to freely give. (Matthew 10:8)

For the remainder of her life (Mother Willer lived to the age of 94), this special lady not only helped her son in his ministry, but she had a ministry of her own: a healing ministry which brought dramatic testimonies throughout north Mississippi and into Tennessee.

As her son's ministry grew, Mother Willer continued to be a part of it. She threw her faith in with the others who were believing for God's best for Mississippi. In the church services, her healing ministry was right alongside that of her son's. Anyone associated with the ministry knew that Pastor Hardy and those close to him, were believing for supernatural healing at every juncture.

From the outset, Pastor Hardy, Sister Ezera, and Mother Willer had looked to God for healing. One of the most dramatic moments came when Hardy, ,Jr. became ill at the age of about 18 months. Several of the praying church members came to the Coleman house and began to intercede for him. He just seemed to be getting sicker by the moment.

They gathered around his bed and anointed him with oil, praying fervently – but nothing seemed to change. He had very high fever and was very weak. Obviously, his life was in danger.

The Colemans' son Jimmy Dee had died at about 14 months, a fact which had brought grave disappointment. Pastor Hardy was distraught that another son was so close to death.

---

*All of the Coleman children learned very early that God would heal them through prayer.*

---

Finally, the Pastor lay down on his bed, turned his face to the wall, and said, "Lord, you know that I'm not kidding. I am really trusting in You." He was praying fervently, and the other prayer warriors were continuing to pray. A couple of hours later, Hardy, Jr.'s fever broke, and suddenly he was totally healed. A miracle had happened.

All of the Coleman children learned very early that God would heal them through prayer. Sometimes they would go to their Dad, and sometimes to their grandmother. They knew that God wanted them healed, and they trusted Him for it.

**Hardy Coleman with his mother Willer and some of the family**

This special lady would boil water and put it in jars. Then she would pray over the water, and often use that in her ministry. In each case she would pray, and follow the leading of the Holy Spirit. The results were awesome. Tumors would disappear. Aches and pains would go. Bones would relocate – you name it.

One time, while farming, a tractor fell on Hardy, Jr.'s foot, crushing it. It was obvious that bones were broken – and the pain was excruciating. The family rushed him to his grandmother's and she began to pray. Mother Willer poured some of her anointed water on the foot, and healing came immediately.

Another time, Mildred had a reaction to a wasp sting, so that her entire face was swollen. Again, she went to her grandmother. Mother Willer first mixed up a paste of milk and powder, and covered Mildred's face. Then she prayed, laying her hands on her granddaughter. Once again, healing came immediately.

A terrific account came from Tonnie Gray, wife of Columbus Gray. I'll share it in her words.

> In 1969 I became pregnant and my husband and I were very excited. However, at the same time, I contracted a serious illness, and we were worried about that – especially since our first son had been stillborn. (We were thinking something could be occurring with the pregnancy). The diagnosis was disturbing: Tuberculosis, with three holes in my lung.
>
> Columbus was very familiar with the ministry of Elder Hardy Coleman, who taught the word of God fervently every chance he got – even at funerals, where he would lead people to the Lord. Every Sunday at Flatwood Grove Church, the members would get up and share their testimonies. So we went to some services.

I heard Mother Willer share the testimony of her healing which she had received the same night she was saved, and she recited the verse, *If there is any sick among you, call for the elders of the church James 5:14-15.* She shared how she was healed without any medication – and her words seemed to come from her heart and settle in my heart. The Lord knew that soon I would need every word.

Doctors advised me to go to a sanitarium in McGee, Mississippi, where I could get the necessary rest and medications for my healing. So my mother-in-law drove me down there, and helped me to get settled in. The prognosis was that it would take me 18 to 22 months for the healing, and that entire time I was to be away from my family and friends. It was all so devastating.

I began to pray as never before. I recalled all of the sermons, songs, and testimonies I had heard, especially those of Mother Willer, and my faith began stirring up to a new level. I wanted God to heal me immediately, but we had to talk first. He had so much to tell me. I committed my life to Him even more than ever; I became imbedded in Christ.

Soon I discovered that the medicine I needed could cause blindness for my unborn child. I remembered Mother Willer saying, "He healed me without medicine." I said, Jesus, do it for me!"

When I had been at the hospital for two and a half weeks, another x-ray was taken of my lungs. The half dollar-sized hole had been healed by a third, and I knew that Jesus was working on it for me. During that time, I could actually feel His hands in mine.

At the end of the third week, I called Columbus to come take me home, even though I hadn't been discharged. I prayed, "God, don't let him ask me if I have been discharged." Thank God, he didn't.

I was still really sick, having lost 15 pounds in the last three weeks. So I rested, but I didn't take the medication. God sent me an angel – my mother-in-law, who cooked for me and sent the siblings to clean my house for me. Four months later, I had gained 40 lbs, and I delivered a 5lb 12oz healthy baby boy – with no problems. Praise be to God.

It has been 45 years, and I have never had a health problem since. No medications, just divine health. I have forgotten which lung was infected, but I have never forgotten the personal relationship Jesus and I shared during the time of my deliverance. Jesus, I will never forget what You have done for me.

> It all started with the faith which was instilled in
> me by the ministry of Elder Coleman and
> Mother Willer.

This healing wasn't just for the Pastor Coleman's family
or for the church. Others who heard testimonies of the
dramatic healings which occurred through Mother
Willer's ministry would seek her out. As a young girl
Mildred remembers cars lined up in front of her
grandmother's house, sometimes extending a block –
people waiting for their turn for prayer. Many were
healed of their diseases.

In one account, a man had migraine headaches which
were disabling. It was suggested that he go to Mother
Willer for healing. She prayed over him, and not much
happened. The next Sunday, Mother Willer looked for
him in church, and he wasn't there. She said, "Today is
his day!" So she went to his house and prayed for him.
Healing came immediately, and he has had no
headaches for 20 years!

Then there was this: a lady had a tumor and came for
prayer. She was healed immediately. Later she passed
the tumor, and sent it to Mother Willer in a jar.
(Mother Willer probably would have preferred a
testimony).

Sometimes people would take their children to her
house to spend the night when they were sick. Just
being in her presence brought healing. Other ministers,

who believed in healing, would go to Mother Willer if they needed healing themselves.

Over the years Mother Willer's faith became so strong that she just couldn't understand doubt. It seemed strange to her that people could believe in God and not believe that He healed. Just as Jesus did, she would "marvel at their unbelief."

---

*Just being in her presence brought healing.*

---

Mother Willer was a remarkable woman of God, a woman of faith, a woman of miracles, and a powerful contributor to the North Mississippi Awakening.

*Thou therefore, my son, be strong in the grace that is in Christ Jesus.*

*II Timothy 2:1*

# 15

## Advice For Young Ministers

My husband, Mickey, and I were sitting in the den at the Colemans' house, visiting as we often had over the last year. The two men had become very close as they had met with other church leaders to pray for the region. Bishop Coleman sat in his chair with my husband close to him, sharing some spiritual thoughts (you know," *iron sharpens iron,"* Proverbs 27:17). Mother Ann sat next to me on the sofa.

I asked a question: "What advice would you like to give to young ministers?" Bishop leaned back in his chair and put his feet up on the ottoman in front of him, pondering.

Mother Ann was the first to reply. "They see the glory, but they don't know the story."

Over the years, the Colemans have had an impact on a large segment of the people in the mid-south region of north Mississippi – and into Tennessee. Many children have grown up listening to this ball-of-fire preacher as he delivered his sermons in person or on TV. They have seen him build church after church – and they have seen the impact his ministry has had.

As a result, dozens have been called into the ministry from within his congregations and from within his own family. A remarkable heritage has been established.

**Bishop Coleman and Mother Ann Renewing Wedding Vows (20th Anniversary)**

Yet often the young ministers don't realize what was involved along the way. The hours of prayer and study. The hours of laboring – when they were already tired.

The disappointments when people would get angry and desert them. The financial sacrifices necessary to keep the ministry going. The perseverance necessary when things got tough.

Bishop chimed in. "Too often young ministers are eager for the title and the position, rather than the work of the ministry. I say that if you are seeking a title, you aren't ready for it yet… When I first got saved, I was just full of joy all the time. Then I found out that the Lord wanted some work , too!" He laughed.

---

## *I tell them to keep it clean.*

---

These are wise people. They have seen young ministers fall into sin because of seeking the position too soon. They get lifted up in pride and fall because of it. (I Timothy 5:22)

So Bishop continued. "I tell them to keep it clean." In other words, stay holy in every aspect of life. That's holiness in your personal life – as well as in the ministry. "I was married to my first wife for 36 years, 6 months, and 3 days, and I was always faithful to her." Before he could go on, Mother Ann spoke up: "Well don't stop now!" They both laughed as he continued, "I've been married to my second wife for 37 years and counting – and I've always been faithful to her, too!"

"I also tell them that the *life you live* preaches to people more than your sermons. If they see you preach one thing and do another, they won't follow you. People will follow your actions more than they follow your words."

**Hardy Coleman and wife Ann with some of the children and grandchildren**

"Shun the very appearance of evil." Several years ago, when there was a drive for black people to vote, an attractive lady who was working with an organization involved in that purpose came to the area, and looked up Bishop (then Elder) Coleman to help her. She knew that he was the primary leader around, and she wanted him to attend a meeting with her to learn about it. Elder Coleman was interested in the mission, but didn't want any misconceptions, so he went with her – but, since his wife couldn't go at the time, had his oldest daughter ride with them. He was absolute in his determination to avoid even the appearance of evil.

That's why so many of Bishop's family members are in the ministry – and successful at it. They have seen this man and woman of God live holy lives – and real lives. They do what they say, living in secret what they preach in public.

"I also tell them that faithfulness is the most important attribute. Success doesn't often come quickly or easily. If you don't stop, you will be successful. You have to stick with it."

"One more slogan I truly believe is, 'Your attitude determines your altitude.'" You have to be positive and full of faith if you are going to do much for God.

---

## *If you don't stop, you will be successful.*

---

Bishop's wisdom continues with more specifics. "When you have new people, don't start preaching about the shortcomings of the church. You have company, so you don't air the family problems. The new people will be discouraged if you do that."

And this: "If you have to bring correction, be as mild as you can. Approach them in a way that they feel love. Take your time. Be careful. Otherwise, they will see the devil before they see Jesus. Think about it as if it were you. You don't want to hurt them when you are trying to lead them to the light." What wisdom!

He continues, "If you have to call a man a dog, call him a *big* dog," chuckling as he spoke. And then more seriously, "And never in front of others. If you can't make an appointment, pull them off to the side for the conversation."

Bishop Coleman and Mother Ann have spent much time fasting and praying. For many years, they fasted every Tuesday and Thursday, and encouraged their people to do the same. They know that there is no substitute for spending time with God. After all, He is the source of all wisdom and strength.

There have been times when people have mistreated the Colemans. Some have "borrowed" money never to repay it. Others have said hurtful things or have jealously tried to tear them down. Some have left in unjustified anger. All of these are hurtful moments which every minister has to go through.

Bishop Coleman has advice for these times also. "When you have been misused, it's more of a blessing to pray for them than for yourself. Sincerely pray for them, and you will forgive them." You are returning good for evil, and God's blessing showers upon you. "Step back and let God take care of it."

And finally, "If you can get people – whether ministers or others – not just thinking about themselves and not exalting themselves, they will be more successful." God Himself is the One who exalts, and that is what has happened to Bishop Coleman.

Bishop has never asked for any promotion he has received. God has exalted him because of his faithfulness to his call.

*God is opposed to the proud, but gives grace to the humble.* (I Peter 5:5)

This grace is more than evident in the lives of Bishop Coleman and Mother Ann.

*For in him we live, and move, and have our being; as certain also of your own poets have said, For we are also his offspring.*

*Acts 17:28*

# 16

## Living Epistles

What's caught is more significant than what is taught. "What you *do* speaks louder than what you *say*." These old adages may be well-worn, but they are true. They are true in raising children, or in training up church members and leaders.

Over the last year, my husband and I have spent many hours in the presence of Bishop Hardy Coleman and Mother Ann. I count that as one of the greatest privileges of my life – to have spent so much time with them. We have attended their meetings, visited with their children and grandchildren, and talked to the pastors in their charge. Many others have volunteered personal testimonies of the life-changing effect of these people.

During the process, I have "caught" lots of observations. Just being in their presence, has allowed me to see the Lord's work in their lives. Of course, I have seen their knowledge of the Word and their ability to communicate it. But there are many ministers who possess those qualities.

What sets these two apart from the crowd is something different. I have seen in their lives many godly characteristics found in the Word – characteristics which could only have come about by years of spending time with Jesus, allowing the Word and the Spirit to mold them into His image.

So I would like to share some of these observations.

> First, there is **Humility**. Clothe yourselves in humility, for it is written: God is opposed to the proud, but gives grace to the humble. Humble yourselves, therefore under the mighty hand of God, and He will exalt you in due time. I Peter 5:5-6

Even though they have influenced thousands, been recognized by crowds, and been elevated to the highest position in their denomination, the Colemans' greatest treasure is their relationship with Jesus. And they give Him all the glory for their success. Bishop's favorite account is still that of his salvation – when he walked down the aisle and received the baptism in the Holy Spirit. "I still get chills thinking about it," he says.

Over the years I have seen ministers who, after they reach a certain amount of success, become unwilling to minister to any individuals. They are for the crowds,

162

but no longer have time for individuals. Not the Colemans.

One lady, who is powerful in the Spirit, shared a special testimony. Several years ago, she was going through some situations which were extremely difficult. In fact, the distress reached such a pitch that one day she found herself crying uncontrollably. The lady went outside and began walking down the street, sobbing. Without even realizing what she was doing, she continued to walk until she came to the Coleman house and went to the door. (They lived in the same neighborhood).

Bishop answered the door and said, "Come in, daughter." Mother Ann was sitting in front of a big basket of peaches, peeling them. Mother Ann then just smiled and greeted her, giving her a knife and a peach. So the lady began peeling also.

---

*There is a time to offer advice,
and a time to be a leaning post.*

---

No one asked what was wrong. They knew the situation. Both of the Colemans began to say things like, "We love you a whole bunch, Sister." And, "Sister, you know that we are here for you." And they continued to peel the peaches.

Just being in their house and in their presence and drawing from their strength helped this  lady make it through. After staying there for awhile, her joy had returned. She knew that her Lord was taking care of the problems. Faith had replaced her grief.

They never asked her to talk about her problems. She says, "There is a time to offer advice, and a time to be a leaning post. The latter is what they were that day." And they seemed to know which she needed at the time.

Then there was a similar testimony, shared by a lady who is now a minister's wife.

This lady had a nervous disorder, causing her great depression. She had been saved for just about a year, and she didn't know what was wrong, or what to do about it. So she called the Colemans, who prayed for her and ministered to her.

Thus began a season of time when this lady would call every day – at noon. It became such a regular event, that the Colemans would try to schedule their activities so that they could be by the phone at noon – for the call. (It was before the time of cell phones). One time the condition seemed so overwhelming that the Colemans went to her house, picked her up, and took her to theirs - putting her into bed until she was better.

Over a period of time, healing came, and the illness was gone. The lady is now a powerful woman of God – and she owes so much of her healing to the tenacity of the Colemans. When she didn't know what to do, they did. And they never gave up until they saw that the healing was complete.

This willingness to take time for the individual is something which was born out of their humility. They see each person as important – just as Jesus does.

> Second is **Holiness**, or Purity. Be holy yourselves in all your behavior, because it is written, "You shall be holy, for I am holy." I Peter 1:15-16

I have already shared about Bishop's marital faithfulness, but there is more to their holiness. It involves the way they live their lives in extreme devotion to the Lord.

When Bishop Coleman first became a bishop and a large sum of money became available to him, he could have justifiably taken some for a salary or expenses. But he didn't. He put every penny, along with some of his own money, into building the Convention Center for his diocese. In fact, even though he personally worked at the endeavor 6 days a week for about 7 months, he never accepted any pay for that. He was pure in his devotion to the cause.

His children speak of the fact that their father was "real." He lived the life at home that he preached about on Sunday. He was full of faith at home – just as he was at church. He was kind to his wife and children at home – just as he was in public.

This holiness is perhaps the major reason so many in his family followed after him. His whole life became a testimony to the reality of Jesus.

> Third is **Faithfulness**. He who is faithful in a very little thing is faithful also in much. Luke 16:10; A faithful man will abound with many blessings. Psalm 28:20

Bishop Coleman has spent 73 years in the ministry. He has grown in his knowledge of the Word and in his ability to deliver it. He has also grown in his reach. Starting out as a preacher on the dirt roads of Benton County, Mississippi, he now has influence which reaches to the entire nation. He has been the speaker at national conventions. He was faithful in little things and now he is faithful in much.

**Global Pacific Diocese Conference, Tupelo MS.**

Every time another opportunity was presented to Bishop Coleman, if he thought it was from the Lord, he would accept it. Bit by bit, year by year, growing in his influence and his reach. Always faithful.

There were times when the faithfulness would be hard. His son, Jimmy Dee died at 14 months. He kept on preaching. There were times when the family was moving, changing farms, or changing occupations. He kept on preaching. His wife of 36 years died. He kept on preaching. Ever faithful to the call.

In 2005, 45 minutes before Bishop Coleman was to deliver the main address to the national convocation of The Church of The Living God, Bishop got the call that his son, Bobby, had just passed away. Drawing on the strength which only comes to those who know their Lord, Bishop delivered the message anyway. Many said that this was the most powerful message they had ever heard him preach.

His daughter, Mildred asked, "Dad, how do you do it?" His reply: "You have to go up higher." You have to go to the place high above this world. The secret place, which only can come from the Holy Spirit indwelling and empowering you.

That's what I call, "faithfulness."

> The fourth **is Diligence**. The hand of the diligent makes rich. Proverbs 10:4; The hand of the diligent will rule. Proverbs 12:24; The soul

of the diligent is made fat. Proverbs 13:4; The plans of the diligent lead to sure advantage. Proverbs 21:5

People mocked. He continued. People said it could never succeed. He continued. Money was scarce. He continued. He worked so hard that he began spitting up blood. He continued.

When Coleman Temple was erected in Ripley, that was what the pastor had to endure. He knew that God's will was for him to build the church and minister to the people, but there was no encouragement from anyone in the neighborhood. Many residents wanted him to go away. (Especially all the drug dealers in the vicinity – and there were many).

Other nay-sayers wondered why he had chosen the worst section of town. Many were afraid to even go into that area. He continued.

## *My Dad is unstoppable.*

For the first year, there were no members. He continued.

Eventually that congregation would foster the development of several ministers with thriving churches of their own. All because of the faithfulness of Bishop Coleman and Mother Ann to press through the obstacles and continue with God's plan.

Oh, and by the way, that most-dangerous area is now considered one of the best neighborhoods in the entire city.

In the words of his son, Junior, "My Dad is unstoppable." He sees obstacles and he faces them head on. If he knows that He is in God's will, he refuses to stop.

If the Colemans had not had diligence, that work of God would not have been done. Against all odds, and in spite of dire circumstances, they completed the assignment God had given them. As a result, hundreds of people came to the Lord – and even the community was changed.

During the writing of this book, I have seen that tenacity with my own eyes. The week before the yearly assembly of the Global Pacific Diocese, Bishop Coleman had to be hospitalized. He was still recovering during that week, but he made every meeting. (There were two a day). For six days, he traveled the 80 mile round trip to be a part of the event, showing encouragement and support for every speaker. He even addressed the crowd himself several times.

He refuses to be stopped.

> Fifth is **Perseverance.** The seed in good soil,
> these are the ones who have heard the Word in
> an honest and good heart, and hold it fast, and
> bear fruit with perseverance. Luke 8:15;
> Perseverance produces proven character, and
> proven character hope, and hope does not
> disappoint. Romans 5:4.

This attribute is similar to diligence, but has a different twist. Diligence implies immediately encountering the obstacles; perseverance implies continuing over a period of time.

In every true ministry, there are times of glory, which almost seem too good to be true. Then there are those other times: when nothing is moving forward. As a minister, you feel like you are treading water. There may be answers to prayer which haven't come yet. There may be problems with people... Things just aren't the way you want them to be.

During those times, perseverance is what you need. And that is certainly one of the attributes of Bishop Coleman.

"Don't quit," says the Bishop. Just keep moving forward, and you will succeed. Even when times are tough, just take one step at a time.

> Finally, they have stayed on the **Path**. In
> Chapter 2, I spoke of two paths mentioned in
> the Bible. Bishop Coleman stayed on the path

of the righteous – which shines brighter and brighter until the noonday sun. The path of life leads upward for the wise. Proverbs 15:24

Proverbs 27:21 says that a man is tested by the praise afforded him. When success comes, then what does he do?

I have seen some who have started out in ministry with a pure heart and right motives. Yet when they began to see some success in their lives, they would change. Pride and self would emerge, and the ministry would take a twist – glorifying the minister, rather than Jesus Himself. Greed or lust would then appear where there had once seemed to be holiness and purity.

Success has not affected Bishop Coleman in a negative way. He seems almost indifferent to the success and attention he has received. Just as he has remained faithful to the Lord, he has remained faithful to the right path.

He hasn't tried to replace the Lord's charge with his own ideas – or ideas which are fashionable. Bishop Coleman and Mother Ann have continued on the righteous path they started from the outset. They have chosen the path of life.

These two, and I'm sure Bishop's first wife Ezera as well, have demonstrated in the totality of their lives what it means to be a disciple of the Lord. They have been living epistles of God's goodness and His grace.

They have been extraordinary people of God.

Bishop Coleman's story is a great story of overcoming odds, but I hope that for you it will be more than that. I hope his story will inspire you to reach for God's highest in your life. There will be disappointments, but he will see you through to victory – if you don't give up.

With faith in the Lord and His Word, with obedience to His leading, and with determination to keep going, you too can have that remarkable life your Creator has planned for you.

Your story will be different, because we are all unique. You have your own personal race to run. It's a race ordained by God, and His empowerment is there for your success.

So go for it! Run that race with faith and vigor. May you too live an extraordinary life.

EXTRAORDINARY

# Appendix A: Churches in the Global Pacific Diocese of the Church of the Living God

At the age of 92, Bishop Coleman still has a robust band of movers and shakers who are running the race with him – ever growing in God's Word and in ministry. If you talk to any of these ministers, you will find that Bishop's encouragement , wisdom, and practical help have made it possible for their success.

## Flatwood Grove Church
## Blue Mountain, Mississippi

**Bishop Hardy Coleman and Mother Ann**

In 1948, Bishop Coleman became pastor of Bald Knob Church, which was meeting in a school building on Hell Creek Road in Blue Mountain. In 1952, when issues arose with the school board, the congregation agreed that it was time for their own building. So the first church building was erected on property owned by two deacons, and the name was changed to Flatwood Grove.

In the early 80's, Flatwood Grove received a facelift – and more, when it was tripled in size. Bishop Coleman led the construction of a new sanctuary, with brick façade and columns. The numbers of believers have continued to grow, as the members assisted with tent meetings and outreaches into the community.

Since 1952, Hardy Coleman, Sr has been pastor of that church. In 2002, Bishop handed over the pastorate of Coleman Temple to a spiritual son, so that today Flatwood Grove is the only one he pastors along with his duties as bishop. Many of Bishop Coleman's children and grandchildren are leaders in this congregation, which has helped him with any thrust of ministry he has pursued.

The Flatwood Grove congregation continues today as the foundation for Bishop Coleman's entire ministry. Dozens of ministers have been raised up in that church – and generations of musicians, prayer warriors, and helps ministers.

They remain the faithful rock in the Global Pacific Diocese of the Church of the Living God.

## Coleman Temple
## Ripley, Mississippi

**Elder Jeremiah Simmons and First Lady Cassandra**

Coleman Temple was a labor of love by Elder Hardy and First Lady Ann Coleman as they envisioned and built the building and began services in 1979. (For the complete story, see Chapter 11). Against great odds, and with little encouragement, the two were determined to build a place for God right in the center of Ripley's most crime-ridden neighborhood.

Since that time, many lives have been transformed by the power of God. Drug dealers, addicts, and others have been gloriously saved and delivered. Over the years, generations of believers have been raise up there – and at least a dozen spiritual sons of Bishop Coleman have entered the ministry. Quite a few of them have started churches of their own, adding to the awakening in the area.

One of Bishop Coleman spiritual sons, Jeremiah Simmons, was an early convert of this mission. From the day he received Jesus and the baptism of the Holy Spirit, this man began winning others to the Lord. His family and friends started coming to the Lord because of his zeal. Interestingly, many people realized that this fireball was called to preach before he did. He just wanted to share Jesus.

Since 2002, Elder Jeremiah Simmons has been pastor of Coleman Temple. Before he became pastor, Elder Simmons was ordained, on the board of the church, and Bishop Coleman right hand man. Today, he serves as a District Elder and State Evangelist for the Global Pacific Diocese.

Elder Simmons and his wife Cassandra still carry the fire of awakening in their ministry, causing their church to thrive. Following in the pattern of Bishop Coleman, the church is filled with generations of their family who are faithfully serving the Lord. They are ministers, musicians, praise leaders, and administrators. It's awesome to see the people – from the grandparents to the tiny children – energetically praising God.

## Mount Olive Church of the Living God
## Memphis, Tennessee

**Elder Terry Macon and First Lady Ida**

Mount Olive was started by two couples: Carey and Linda Williams and Marion and Annell Brown as a home Bible study. In 1983 it seemed time to take the ministry to the next level, so the couples rented a small one-room building on Mount Olive Street (Thus the name), and began having services there. At that time they solicited the help of Elder Hardy Coleman and Mother Ann.

Chapter 12 goes into the founding of Mount Olive in great detail, so here we will just give highlights. After a couple of years, the ministry was growing and they needed more room. At the same time, a building came up for sale on Tchulahoma Avenue. It was a large, beautiful facility and the odds were that this would be impossible for them to purchase. God's favor prevailed, however, and the building became theirs – much to everyone's delight.

During those early years, Elder Coleman served as pastor to Mount Olive – as well as his two Mississippi churches. The Flatwood Grove congregation pitched in to help with ministers, musicians, and worship leaders. Deciding that the congregation needed a pastor who was on site, Elder Coleman turned the leadership over to a local pastor in the late 80's.

Today Elder Terry Macon and his wife are the pastors of Mount Olive. Elder Macon is a second cousin to Bishop Coleman, and has benefitted from the mentorship of this great man. Under the leadership of Elder and First Lady Macon, the church continues to thrive.

## Red Oak Grove Church Of The Living God
## Okolona, Mississippi

**Elder Henry Jeans and
First Lady Luberta**

Elder Henry Jeans became pastor of Red Oak Grove Church in 1980, the same year that Elder Hardy Coleman joined the Church of the Living God and became District Elder. This was to be a long term relationship as these two spiritual giants formed a powerful bond, and have shared a wealth of knowledge. When the Bishop Coleman organized the Global Pacific Diocese, Elder Jeans joined, and has been a District Elder – and the State Elder for Mississippi.

Bishop Coleman has not only provided spiritual assistance to red oak Grove, but natural as well. In 1986 and 1987, Bishop Coleman contractor's skills allowed him to help add some construction to the existing Red Oak Grove building. He helped expand the sanctuary, added a foyer with men's and women's bathrooms, and added a new roof.

In 2001, this church joined the Global Pacific Diocese under the leadership of Bishop Hardy Coleman, Sr.

Red Oak Grove and the pastor, Elder Henry Jeans have been true rocks in the diocese, helping Bishop Coleman keep it strong and moving forward.

## New Birth Outreach
## for Deliverance Ministries
## Chicago, Illinois

*In the words of Elder Samuel Hunter:*

**Illinois State Elder Hardy L Coleman Jr. and First Lady Lois**

Before the foundation of the world, God looked and saw that in the last days perilous times would come, and without direction His people would rush toward the end of time to eternal damnation. So for the purpose of a dynamic end-time ministry, on June 21, 1951 in Ashland, Mississippi, Hardy Lee Coleman, Jr. was born. From his conception, God began to prepare him for a great work, and the course of events in his life began to shape the ministry of New Birth

Outreach for Deliverance Ministries in Chicago, Illinois.

In 1977, Hardy L. Coleman, Jr. married his soul mate, the beautiful Lady Lois Coleman. Together they would establish the future of the vision handed down from the Most High God.

Hardy L. Coleman, Jr. confessed his calling into the ministry in 1984 at Coleman Temple in Ripley, Mississippi. Shortly thereafter, in 1986, he took on the mantle of pastor. While reading the book, "The Pastor's Handbook," the words appeared, "You will build a church and the name will be New Birth." Thus the inception of our ministry was revealed, and we began this new work in Chicago.

Beginning humbly, we moved three times in the early years. As Pastor Coleman taught under the mighty anointing of the Holy Spirit, in meetings and on television, our ministry began to bear fruit, and many were added to the church. To accommodate our now-growing ministry, once again we moved to the auditorium of the Maranatha Christian Academy located on West 108th Street in Chicago.

In November 2000, while holding revival in his hometown in Mississippi, Pastor Coleman received new instructions. In a state between sleep and wakefulness, the Pastor had a visitation from the Lord. The Lord showed the

Pastor that this is a new beginning, and began to give new instructions for the ministry. Always obedient to the Lord, Pastor Coleman began to hand down these valuable instructions for life straight from the Master's throne. His mission: to transform dysfunctional people into functional sons in the Kingdom of God.

With this new vision in hand, Pastor Coleman and the constituents of New Birth Outreach for Deliverance Ministries stepped out on pure faith and purchased our first edifice located in Chicago Heights, Illinois at 711 West 15$^{th}$ Street.

Although we at New Birth Ministries are extremely excited about this new move of God, this is only the beginning of our story. Eye hath not seen, nor ear heard, neither hath entered into the heart of man, the things which God hath prepared for them that love him. I Corinthians 2:9

The best is yet to come!

## Greater Spring Hill Toccopola
## Thaxton, Mississippi

**Elder Wylie Starks and**
**First Lady Freedia**

Greater Spring Hill Toccopola was established in 1905, so it's the oldest church in the diocese. There have been many bishops and elders over the years, but the mission of holiness – and reaching out to the community have never waned.

In 2002 Elder Wylie Starks, nephew of Bishop Coleman, took over as pastor, under the leadership of Bishop Coleman. With Elder Starks as pastor,, the people have developed a sense of unity which is not often seen in churches. The congregation is small, but powerful. They understand the principle that in working together, they can get the job done. They try to meet the natural as well as spiritual needs of the community.

Elder Starks is a prayer warrior, and one who seeks the Holy Spirit for leading and manifestation among the people. He prays the prayers of Paul over the church – especially those found in Ephesians 1 and 3– that their spiritual eyes may be opened, they be filled with a knowledge of His will, come to know His love, and be filled up to the fullness of God. No wonder the congregation is in unity and growing in their service to the Lord. It's a wonderful work of the Holy Spirit.

## Chapel Grove Holiness Church
## Chesterville, Mississippi

**Elder Garnie Freeman and First Lady Adonna**

The oldest church in the diocese is Chapel Grove, which was founded by Elder Ollie Robins, in the 1940's. Starting in a small one-room building on County Line Road, he later moved the congregation to a small frame building out in the woods. During that phase, the members would have to ride in their wagons through dust and mud in order to get to church. Yet they still came to hear the powerful word of God being preached by Elder Robins.

The second phase of the church came when Pastor Johnny Jenkins became the leader. While he was there, the frame building burned down. At that time, 18 acres of land were donated to the church by Sister Loubether Satterwhite Hadley, and the members built a new building.

In 1950, Elder George T. Howell became pastor, and continued for 45 years. He was a strong leader and led many to the Lord. A year after he left, in 1995, Elder Garnie Lee Freeman, who had been mentored by Elder Howell, became pastor.

Today, Elder Freeman continues as pastor. Having grown up in the congregation, and having been mightily filled with the Holy Spirit, Elder Freeman leads with vision and purpose.

## Richardson Chapel Holiness Church
## Guntown, Mississippi

**Elder Leo Robins and First Lady Annie**

Richardson Chapel was founded in a place called McGee by Pastor Jean Rapier, Bishop G.T. Howell, and Bishop Ollie Robins. The first building was a wooden school building, which was turned into a church. It was part of the revival which brushed across north Mississippi in the mid 20th century. Many were baptized in the Holy Spirit and dedicated to a life of holiness.

The current pastor is Elder Leo Robins, son of Bishop Ollie Robins. Bishop Robins was the bishop who preceded Bishop Coleman as territory leader for the Church of the Living God.

Elder Robins has been dedicated to the Lord since his youth, and is known as a mighty prayer warrior. Elder Robins, assistant pastor Elder Sammie L. Staples, and First Lady Annie L. Robins continue to lead the congregation with passion and purpose.

## New Hope In Christ Healing Ministries
## Chicago, Illinois

**Elder Gail Williams with husband Deacon K.C.**

Elder Gail Williams and her husband, Deacon K.C., started New Hope In Christ Healing Ministries in their living room in 2002. Over the years it has grown, so that they have turned their basement into a sanctuary. The seating, worship instruments, and podium accommodate the members who attend. Today, about 35 members meet there regularly.

Evangelism and prayer are the two major thrusts of this ministry. There are many prayer warriors and street ministers in the group, and with that combination, they are making a difference in the lives of those around them.

## Ministry of the Lost Sheep
## Shannon, Mississippi

**Elder Maurice Loving and First Lady Mary**

In 2009, God gave Elder Maurice Loving a vision of building a church to minister to those who were lost. The vision was that this building would be debt free – built with his own hands, and financed by the Lord as he proceeded.

Though many said this couldn't be done, Bishop Coleman was very excited. He had a witness to the venture – and even seeded some of his own money into the project. So with that confirmation, Elder Loving began to build. Frequently, during the building process, Bishop Coleman would call and check on Elder Loving, giving him encouragement – and additional finances on occasion.

On the fourth Sunday in March, 2013, the building was finished, and the church held its first meeting. Just as envisioned, the church is debt-free.

The vision of Elder Loving now is to go into the highways and byways and search for the lost sheep. There are many out there who need for Jesus to deliver them as only He can. This church is making a difference for God's Kingdom.

## Judah House of Praise
## Atlanta, Georgia

**Elder Carey Williams and First Lady Linda**

Elder Carey and Linda Williams were some of the founders of Mount Olive Church in Memphis, Tennessee. A few years later, when Elder Carey was transferred to the Atlanta area, they started a Bible study in their home, and quickly began to realize that they were called to organize another church. In August of 1998, with Isaiah 61:1-3 as their foundational scripture, Elder Williams named the church Judah House of Praise, and a new work began.

As the numbers grew, it was time to rent a building, which they did for two years. At the end of that time, the owner wanted to sell the property, but the no one in the congregation had enough money to buy it – or the means to borrow enough money.

Of course, Elder Carey and Linda began to pray – along with others in their congregation. At one such meeting, an unassuming lady surprised them by saying, "I know some people with money." She subsequently introduced them to some wealthy investors – and eventually they made the purchase. The landlord then knocked off $17,500.00 from the rent they had paid – to go toward the down payment. At closing, the church had to pay only $32.74 in order to purchase the $300,000 building. Only God could pull that one off!

In July, 2008, Judah House of Praise joined the Church of the Living God under Bishop Hardy Coleman. They have continued to teach the Word of God, to praise, to pray, and to help their congregation grow in the attributes of God. They also have continued to see God's mighty hand through miraculous healings and deliverances.

Judah House of Praise is continuing to impact their neighborhood – in this suburb of Atlanta.

**Wilson Chapel**

**New Albany, Mississippi**

**Elder Troy Starks and the late First Lady Carolyn**

Wilson Chapel has an interesting history. It was named for Pastor Dewey Wilson, who pastored the church for many years. Although he went on to be with the Lord in the late 80's, his wife lived much longer. First Lady Betty Wilson passed away in 2006 at the age of 116 years. (At the time of her death, she was listed as the 4th oldest person in the world).

My husband and I visited Miss Betty shortly before her death, and she was quick to share her salvation experience at the age of 12. (She had been saved for 104 years). Her memory was waning in certain areas, but that one event was crystal clear. In fact, she attributed her long life to her relationship with the Lord. Quite a lady!

For the last 27 years, Wilson Chapel has been under the leadership of Elder Troy Starks, a nephew of Bishop Coleman. First Lady Carolyn Starks passed away in 2013, but she was very instrumental in the leadership of the church.

Elder Starks and his wife took Wilson Chapel to a new level of evangelism. They purchased vans, and began providing transportation for those who needed a ride to church. Their special emphasis was the children from the poor sections whose parents didn't attend.

The generous First Lady Carolyn would often pick up the children and take them to her house before church. There she would give them breakfast, baths, and new clothes before taking them to learn about their Savior. She was truly a woman of compassion.

Today Elder Starks continues with the bus ministry. Not only children, but others who need a ride are brought to the church to hear God's Word and learn of His Holy Spirit.

Under the leadership of Elder Starks and Bishop Coleman, Wilson Chapel has continued to flourish.

## Because Of Grace Church
## New Albany, Mississippi

**Elder Adrian Ivy**

Because Of Grace Church was founded by Elder James Gray under the name of The Potter's House. After pastoring the church for about four years, he resigned, and only a few people remained.

It dwindled to the point where only Deacon Charlie McKenzie and Sister Tonnie Gray were there. These two were sure that the Lord wanted to continue the work, so they faithfully prayed for direction.

Sister Tonnie Gray is a counselor, and while attending an American Association of Christian Counselors conference in Nashville, she was greatly impacted. The word, "grace" kept ringing in her spirit, even as she drove back to New Albany. All she could think about was how loaded that word was, and what it had done for her personally. She began to hear the words, "Because Of Grace."

Returning home, Sister Tonnie went to Deacon McKenzie and shared with him. She thought they needed to change the name of the church to Because Of Grace. He was elated. They needed a fresh start, and he had a witness in his spirit that this was from God. So they changed the name.

Today, the church is under the pastorship of Elder Adrian Ivy, and under the leadership of Bishop Coleman. It is growing, and the future is looking bright. They are reaching out to others to bring them into God's grace, and helping them to grow in Christ.

---

These are the churches which are currently in the Global Pacific Diocese and under the leadership of Bishop Coleman. Over the years, he has had influence in many other churches and with many pastors – helping them to grow in their knowledge of God. His influence has been so broad that it truly cannot be measured.

EXTRAORDINARY

# Appendix B: Comments

*These comments made by ministers, family, and friends will give you more insight into the lives of Bishop Coleman and Mother Ann. They will continue to show lives well-lived. They will also show lives well-balanced. They have been very busy for God – but they always have had time for their children and grandchildren. Read on, and you will see for yourself.*

## Elders and Ministers

When we first heard of a book being written on Bishop Coleman's life nothing but joy filled our hearts. This is truly a well-deserved honor for Bishop Coleman and his family.

As I think back through the years of our relationship I remember well the year I was appointed Pastor of the Red Oak Grove Church. It was around 1980, the same year Elder Hardy Coleman, Sr. was appointed to be Red Oak Grove's District Elder. During those remarkable years a wonderful bond was formed and a wealth of knowledge was shared. Bishop Coleman, then District Elder Coleman, not only helped guide the church spiritually, but also he helped naturally. Between 1986 and 1987, he used his contractor skills to expand the sanctuary, to add a foyer to house a men and women's bathroom, and to add a new roof. The members of Red Oak Grove Church are very proud to have been taught and touched by such a great, extraordinary man of God.

Bishop Coleman, May God continue to shine his face upon you and bless you.

**Mississippi State Elder Henry Jeans**
Red Oak Grove Church
Okolona, Mississippi

Since he is my father, Bishop Coleman has been my example and my mentor all of my life. He has lived the life that represents complete faithfulness to Jesus Christ, not only at church, but also at home.

My Dad is unstoppable. Whenever challenges would come, he would meet them head on. Then he would keep going strong.

It has been an honor to be his son.

**Illinois State Elder Hardy L. Coleman, Jr.**
New Birth Outreach for Deliverance Ministries
Chicago, Illinois

For the last 34 years, ever since I got saved, Bishop Coleman has been my mentor and my friend. I started out as a new believer, and his teaching and example have helped me to grow to become a minister – and eventually to become the Pastor of Coleman Temple.

My entire family has been blessed by Bishop Coleman and Mother Ann. I praise God everyday for these wonderful people of God.

**District Elder Jeremiah Simmons**
Coleman Temple
Ripley, Mississippi

My congregation, my wife, and I are very thankful for Bishop Hardy Coleman and for his unselfish acts of love for the churches in our diocese. We are also thankful for Mother Ann and his family, for they have been willing to share Bishop Coleman with us.

I have been blessed in that Bishop Coleman is my uncle as well as my bishop. Therefore, I have been able to learn from the natural as well as the spiritual aspects of his life. This relationship has been a source of strength and encouragement during his years as my mentor. His leadership has been of great value when faced with difficult situations. I am very thankful for the leading of the Holy Spirit, but sometimes, it's nice to have someone who can lead by example to talk to.

**District Elder Wylie Starks**
Greater Spring Toccopola
Church of the Living God
Thaxton, Mississippi

Bishop Coleman is an awesome man of God. He is very humble and easy to relate to. He knows his pastors and always encourages us to be moral, preach the word, and keep our charge. My wife and I love him dearly, and pray God continues to bless him and his wife.Elder Maurice lovingMinistry of the Lost SheepOkolona, Mississippi

I thank God for an anointed Bishop. He is one who is faithful, and has been a great blessing to me.

**Elder Gail P. Williams**
New Hope in Christ Healing Ministries
Chicago, Illinois

I have known Bishop Coleman all of my life, since he was a friend of my father's. He is a hard worker in the church, and an excellent prayer partner.

**Elder Leo Robins**
Richardson Chapel Holiness Church
Guntown, Mississippi

Bishop Coleman is always encouraging and always full of spiritual advice. I know that I can call him anytime. He and my mother have made a great couple.

**First Lady Linda Williams**
Judah House of Praise
Atlanta, Georgia

As his nephew and a Pastor under his leadership, Bishop Coleman has meant so much to me. He has shared his wisdom and his encouragement throughout the 27 years that I have pastored under him.

**Elder Troy Starks**
Wilson Chapel
New Albany, Mississippi

Bishop Coleman is a great man of God! He has always been ready to assist our church in any way that he could. I am thankful to be serving under his leadership.

**Elder Garnie Lee Freeman**
Chapel Grove Holiness Church
Chesterville, Mississippi

Bishop Coleman is very special to me. He has always taught the Word of God fervently, and that helped me to get my healing.

**Tonnie Gray**
Because of Grace Church
New Albany, Mississippi

Bishop Coleman and Mother Ann have been like a mother and father to me. They have been there in the spiritual and in the natural – to guide and encourage me in every situation. I have nothing but praise for them – and the way they have lived their lives.

**Minister Annette Gray**
Mississippi State Secretary
Global Pacific Diocese

# Children

My father is totally real. That quality has always made me aware of the reality of God and His place in our lives. We learned from an early age that if we would put God and His Word first place, He would bless us.

### Lottie Clarke, Daughter

My father and my mother were truly kind and respectful of each other. That unconditional love they showed was an example for us to follow. We learned very early what a godly family was all about.

### Mildred Chills, Daughter

We learned at a very early age that we should take our needs to prayer. We had a family prayer time every day. We would gather around and ask God for our needs to be met. And they were!

### Dwight Coleman, Son

Even though my father was busy working and ministering, we always knew that we were the most important people to him. His watchful eye was always there – protecting us and training us because of his love.

### Carnelia Barnes, Daughter

Our father has been our role model – in our childhood and in our adult lives. He is the greatest man of God I have ever known, and his example has continued to guide me throughout my life.

### Mary Ruth Nesbit, Daughter

I am so happy that my Mother and Bishop Coleman have each other. They are two of God's finest people. They love the Lord and are sold out – rooted and grounded in God's Word. As they lead by example, they are fine examples of the fruit of the Spirit, and God's favor.

### Louise Williams, Daughter

I am so thankful to my mother for bringing up all of her children in the church and with good values. It was instilled in us to be obedient, love one another, treat everyone with respect, and most importantly to keep God first.

### Linda Williams, Daughter

I remember standing by a tree alone at the Harris family picnic. It was my first family event, and I was quiet and shy, even though I was excited to be there. Paw-Paw came over to me with a smile and said, Hi, Daughter. I was an only child, so I don't like seeing someone standing alone."

Bishop Coleman has been such a wonderful man to all of our family. He's kind, giving, and has set an example for our boys to grow up as Christian men…Mother has always put her family first. My college education came through great sacrifice to her…but that's the way she was. I love them both.

### Elaine Wherry, Daughter

Paw-Paw then talked to me about his life growing up as a child, making sure that he included the day he got saved. That was the first time I heard some of Paw-Paw-s life stories, and I loved hearing them. That day he made me feel loved, and he still does. I love him, too.

### Shirley Harris

# Grandchildren

My Grandpa is my ROCK. He has been that since I have known him. He has created a generation of pastors, missionaries, prophets, and saints. I give him the highest respect and love him with all my heart.
Who am I? His eldest granddaughter. I love you papa!

### Pamela Lockhart

My grandfather is a great man of God. I want to be able to be like he is in the kingdom. He is one of the best things in my life.

### Eric Johnson

I think papa Coleman is the manifestation of the love of God on Earth.

### Kathy Johnson (Eric's Wife)

My papa is great. I never have seen him do anything bad or unfair to anybody, - family or otherwise. He is a great man. Besides Jesus, he is the "man."

### Gill Johnson

The greatness of a man can always be measured by his willingness to be kind. Papa is kind, loving, humble, caring, and has a vision beyond belief. Love this wonderful man.

### Carla Johnson (Gill's wife)

If it weren't for my grandfather, I don't think we would be the people we are and where we are. He instilled a lot of great values into his family.

### Gary Johnson

My grandfather loves people and all he wants to see is people saved. That's his #1 priority and it does not matter whether they are family or not. He is a true apostle who loves souls.

## Jeff Johnson

My Papa has set the pace for me in many areas of my life. He is a road map to many of life's challenges: from preaching, to keeping a family together, to working hard to have a great life. Papa is a pattern for young boys trying to become great men and fathers.

## Detrick Johnson

Papa is a great man of God - with a big heart for people and love for spreading God's Word and growing God's Kingdom! I have only known him for 6 months, but he and Grandma Ann have welcomed me and shown me love. I feel as if I've known him all my life. He is a special person.

## Angie Johnson (Detrick's wife)

My grandfather is a man I have respected ever since I was a child. Now that I am a grown woman that respect lives on. When he comes to Illinois for a visit, or when I am in Mississippi, he shows so much love - not only to me, but to his entire family, to all our friends, and to strangers he has never met. That's the grandfather I love. Love you papa!

## Wendy Barnes

I love my grandfather. He is a great and honorable man.

### Deon Carruth

As a child I knew if anyone was living a saved and upright life, it was Papa because he demonstrated it every day in his life.

### Devon Nesbit

My grandfather is and has always been a great man and an awesome man of God.

### Edward Coleman

My grandfather has proven that which is true, that a committed life to God will not fail you in this life or the next. His love for God and people has been a blessing to him and to those who come into contact with him. We love you PAPA, and we will make you proud!

### LaToya Laws and Family

My granddad is an honest, hardworking man... who believes in treating people fair. He has been there any time I needed him. He pushes living a moral life, and he has served GOD practically all of his life. He has instilled morals and the importance of church in me.

### Corey Chills

I enjoy living across the street from Papa. I remember the days when he would ride Annija, our daughter, around in the basket of his bike. He is a blessing to us and we love him very much. He always shares his wisdom and I appreciate i

**Tasha Chills (Corey's Wife)**

My grandfather is a very courageous man. He taught us to stay humble, never give up, and always get up and try again. He set a well-lit path for us to follow. But we ALL know it's impossible to fill his shoes. Thank you, Papa, for the drive you placed in each one of us.

**Fallon Rakestraw**

Papa is a hard worker. He knows what he wants, and he knows what it takes to get. He's thoughtful too. He always had a tip for me when I was doing well in school or life. It wasn't about the money, though. Most people wouldn't care enough to acknowledge it, but he always recognized hard work. I guess he saw a little of himself in me.

**Tyler Chills**

My great grandfather is just what the name says, "Great." When God created him, He broke the mold. He is a true example of a man and man of God. He has instilled in all of us how to be true men and women of God. I believe that he has assisted in establishing a remnant of men and women who will stand and fight till the end, because that is just who he is and what he has accomplished. Papa, we will make sure you finish your course strong, and we will carry on to be great men and women like you. I love my Papa!!

### Bridget Hill

He is one of the greatest men I have ever known.

### Willie Hill, Jr. (Bridget's Husband)

When Bishop Coleman married my grandmother, we asked him if we could call him Paw Paw. Of course, he said, "yes," and he has been the best Paw Paw ever. He always taught us that it was important for us to have good morals and values.

One summer I came to Blue Mountain to visit. My cousin, Pam, was already driving, so she drove us to Aunt Lottie's in Paw Paw's car, and let me drive back home. As I was driving, I sideswiped a truck parked on the side of the road, and was I terrified to tell Paw Paw he had a dent in his car! All he said was, "That's okay, Baby. Those things happen...I'm glad you are okay." Whew! I knew at that moment that he had unconditional love for me.

Mother and Paw Paw give from their hearts. You will never hear them raise their voices at each other – or at others. Their lives are authentic – and cannot be duplicated.

### Angela "Angie" Cage

I am so thankful to have such a beautiful, sweet, loving grandmother who has shown her grandchildren how to live for the Lord. She has taught us how to be respectful and kind to one another. (She also has taught us how to cook).

Paw Paw is such a strong, loving, kind man of God. He built so many churches, always loving his work for the Lord. Because of his faithfulness to God, his family, and his ministry, he has been blessed tremendously.

My grandmother and Paw Paw have impacted my life forever.

**Tereca Williams**

I am blessed to have the best grandparents anyone could wish for. They are so full of wisdom, unconditional love – and laughter. Some of my favorite memories are spending time with my grandparents, aunts, uncles, and cousins. When we are together, there is always fun and laughter.

**Charisse Brown**

My Paw Paw always carried some Doublemint Gum, and he would share it with us when we saw him. On one occasion, when I was a toddler, he offered it, but my Mom wouldn't let me have it. Apparently, I pitched a fit about it, and my Paw Paw never forgot it. He still reminds me of that day, and laughs about it. With so many cousins and other family, it's amazing to me that he remembers that incident so well.

### Cher Rhonda Brown

Not too long ago, my Paw Paw and I went to Walmart. It was just the two of us, and I enjoyed talking with him one-on-one – with no one to interrupt. He showed me different areas of Blue Mountain, and had a story for each one.

When we arrived at Walmart, so many people stopped him to talk. It is obvious that he is admired and respected by many people who know him.

### Kedra Wherry

As one of his grandsons and ordained elders, I am proud to call Paw Paw my grandfather. I have always admired his diligence in ministry and his love for his family. Even when I was a small child, Mother Coleman and Paw Paw made me feel included, important, and loved. These wonderful people have given us a legacy and a heritage of godly living and family values. Our families have been blessed tremendously as a result of their wonderful lives.

### Jherald Williams

I have the best grandparents, because they have set the example for how a family should be. I've witnessed firsthand the love, time, and dedication they've given to our family, the church, and others. Regardless of the situation, I have never seen them out of character –

always kind and sweet. I am blessed and honored to have them as my grandparents.

### Cedric Williams

Paw Paw is known for building up his churches and pastoring them with great knowledge. Mother is known for her old country homemade biscuits.

### Pastor Corey Williams

My grandmother is the sweetest ever. She always has a smile, and nobody can fix banana pudding or homemade biscuits like she can!

### Corey Williams, Jr.

About two years ago, while I was visiting Blue Mountain, Paw Paw asked me a computer question, so we went to the computer. He started navigating through screens and putting a sermon together. I am somewhat of a computer nerd, and I was impressed that this man born in horse and buggy days, knew as much about a computer as I did.

### Garick Wherry

Mother and Paw Paw are the greatest grandparents. Paw Paw always speaks words of wisdom and encouragement… and Mother could sell her recipes for her famous banana pudding and biscuits.

**Brian Williams**

As I was growing up, some of my most memorable moments were watching my Paw Paw preach. When I was a teenager, our church put on a play, and I was asked to play the preacher. When the part came for me to "preach," I tried to act like him, using his style as a guide…The play was a success, and I had lots of compliments on my "sermon."

**Eric Wherry**

EXTRAORDINARY

# About the Author

I'm Suellen Estes, wife of a remarkable husband, mother of four amazing children (all with equally amazing spouses), grandmother of 13 (yes, 13) incredible grandchildren, author, and a speaker with a heart for awakening in America.

For the last 21 years, I have assisted my husband in pastoring Life Connection Church in Blue Mountain, Mississippi. Together we have seen many lives changed and delivered by the power of God's love and His Word.

Recently there has been a shift in my mission. With the world in crisis, I am hearing the call for "all hands on deck." There are many Christians who have a message in their hearts, but no platform for delivering it. Perhaps it's a message to teenagers, or singles, or married couples, or ministers, or... you get the point.

Remarkably, we have at our hands just the means to get these messages out... and at a cost which is next to nothing. That amazing alternate universe, otherwise known as the digital world, is beckoning us all to take our messages to the internet through writing books and blogs, or through speaking on podcasts and teleseminars. Even video is available to those who choose.

The secret is in learning how to use these technologies, and that's what my mission is all about. I have started a website webministrysuccess.com, which is all about learning and using the techniques available. I have come to know many experts in this field, and I am going to be sharing their information with you. There will be regular podcasts in which the specialists will share their knowledge.

I hope you will join me. The world needs Jesus and His Word, just as we do. So help me take the message to them. Hope to see you soon!

http://webministrysuccess.com
suellen@webministrysuccess.com

# Forever Upward

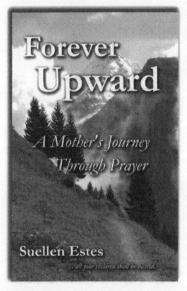

Do you sometimes feel overwhelmed because you know that "things just aren't right" with your children?

I often speak at women's conferences and at the end of the sessions pray with individuals. 75% of the prayer requests are concerning children – often teens and adults. I see panic in their eyes as these mothers share their fears. Often times, they have given up hope of any sort of normal life for their offspring. Drugs, alcohol, and other wrong choices have taken their toll.

Yet There Is Hope! Even more than that, There Are Promises of Transformation!

## Prayer Can Accomplish Incredible Change In The Lives Of Your Children!

When I say, "Prayer," I don't mean just some desperate cries for help. I mean prayer the way God planned it, as outlined in His Word. He gives us insight. He gives us faith. He gives us the power to accomplish His will.

In Forever Upward, you will go on a journey, traveling the path that many mothers have taken before you. It's a journey of hope and a journey of deliverance. You will learn that when you do things God's way, you will have God's results!

To obtain your copy of this book go to
http://foreverupward.com